T␣␣␣
DAILY BREW

*A 365-Day
Guided Journal*

**Maria Pita, BA
Morgan DeSimone, BA
Gary Robinson, LMHC**

outskirts
press

Credits

The authors wish to thank Dan Gilbert, without whose generosity this project would not have been possible. They also would like to extend their appreciation to the following people who reviewed the final manuscript and offered their expertise and guidance in making *The Daily Brew Journal* the best resource it can possibly be for its readers: Laura Maneates, Sydney Scalici, Victoria Tarbell, Authern Xu and Meghan Dushko.

A special thanks to Sandy Rorick for her technical assistance, Monica Calzolari for her marketing expertise, and Karen McGrath for her support and encouragement.

An additional thanks goes out to Hartwick College in Oneonta, NY (www.hartwick.edu) for allowing us to use their facilities, staff time and support in the development of *The Daily Brew Journal.*

Finally, we would like to recognize the important contributions of the "Fifty-Fifty" Peer Counseling Program at Hartwick College: Cilina Jagrup, Sofie Brennan, Tyler Fish, Laura Agnew, Jessica Grima, and Nicole Paladino.

Dedication

*This book is dedicated to the students,
faculty and staff of Hartwick College.*

HARTWICK
COLLEGE

est. 1797

Dear *Daily Brew Journal* Owner:

Congratulations on your commitment to bettering yourself by using our 365-day guided journal! We think if you dedicate even as little as 10 minutes a day, within a short time you will begin to notice the benefits.

A number of scientific studies have found that journaling provides some really cool, unexpected benefits:

- Increases in emotional intelligence
- Gains in short and long-term memory
- Better ability to document progress in achieving important life goals
- Help with impulse control and problem solving
- Improvements in creativity, self-awareness and confidence

Another amazing outcome in the lives of people who commit to the self-discipline of regular journaling is a reduction in their daily stress levels and a lower tendency to "bottle" emotions. "Bottling" emotions is connected to symptoms of anxiety and depression and journaling is, in our opinion, one of the best ways to avoid this tendency.

In our fast-paced, stress-filled world, it has become commonplace to hear people say, "I have too much on my plate" or, "I spend too much time in my head over-thinking my problems". Since you can never write as fast as you can think, journaling slows things down and lets you reflect on your thoughts, emotions and behaviors. When you do that, it helps you to see things going on in your life more objectively and increases your tolerance for the unpredictability which is a normal part of living. In short, people who regularly journal are often less stressed and more productive.

When you begin to examine *The Daily Brew Journal* you'll notice how most of the pages have a little steaming cup in the upper right hand corner next to the words *Daily Brew*. These pages mostly ask you to think about a prompt that we provide at the top of the page and then write a response on the lines provided. Occasionally, we mix it up and encourage you to do some coloring, attempt a word search game, etc. The other pages have a graphic of a person walking next to the words *Daily Do*. These pages challenge you to actively try a new behavior before writing a brief description of the experience. You can choose which type of experience you feel you have the energy for or interest in on a particular day; you don't have to follow a step-by-step path from Day 1 to Day 365. If you skip around, it will still produce the same benefits. The only thing besides a pen or pencil you'll need to effectively use *The Daily Brew Journal* is a set of colored pencils or crayons for those pages asking you to color or draw something.

Notice that we didn't date the pages so if you miss a day or two, no big deal. Just pick up where you left off; you can date the pages to keep track of how often you journal if you wish. Dating the pages also may give you insights later into how you were thinking or feeling during a particular time period in the past. While we recommend doing a "page-a-day", we understand that when schedules get busy it's harder to accomplish this. No worries, just keep carrying on; our 365-day journal may take you a good bit more than a year to finish and that's ok! Even if you don't write anything in your journal on a particular day, it may be a good idea to read a couple of the thought-provoking quotes found on the bottom of each page. This may inspire you to re-think a problem, get creative and have a better day than you would otherwise have had. There's a ton of collective wisdom on these pages that might come in handy in ways that you never expected! If you check out the last pages of the book, you'll see that we added several *Notes* pages with lines in case you need extra space to go into detail on any of the 365 daily prompts or want to jot down an idea, a to-do list or just need room for random free writing.

Don't worry about spelling and punctuation — remember, this is your personal journal, not a graded homework assignment. No one else but you should see your responses (unless you choose to share them with a trusted friend) so there should be no holding back for fear of judgement while you write. Respond to the prompts as quickly as you can as this taps into your creative side and allows for a free association of ideas. Keep your journal in a safe, private place (perhaps even in a bag or backpack so you can do mobile journaling from time to time) and remind yourself that the most important rule of journaling is that there are no rules of journaling.

Why do we recommend journaling with your favorite hot beverage? Because many scientific studies point to generally positive effects of drinking tea, coffee or even cocoa in moderation. Drinking a hot beverage, in general, is a soothing activity that goes well with reflecting and writing about your experiences in *The Daily Brew Journal*. If caffeine affects you negatively with anxiety, insomnia, restlessness or irregular heartbeat, the good news is that each of these beverages have de-caffeinated options. Various studies have found that coffee and tea are high in antioxidants and these may reduce the risk of some cancers. Moderate use of coffee or tea stimulates brain activity and may help protect against dementia, Alzheimer's disease and Parkinson's disease.Similarly, they may lower one's risk for type 2 diabetes and cardiovascular disease. Coffee and particularly white and green tea can help boost the immune system. For people looking to lose a few pounds, moderate coffee or tea drinking may be of assistance. These drinks can boost metabolic rate by up to 10 percent and, coupled with exercise and a nutritious diet, can be a part of a successful weight-management program. As one of many approaches to a healthy lifestyle, coffee and tea in moderation have undeniable benefits.

Lastly, no journal is a substitute for an in-person counselor if your life is so stressful that things are beginning to consistently affect your day-to-day "functioning": sleep, appetite, mood, attitude, ability to concentrate, etc. If this is the case, journaling is a nice supplement to counseling and therapy but not a replacement. Don't hesitate to reach out for help; it's a sign of strength, not weakness!

It is our sincere hope that *The Daily Brew Journal* will become a part of your routine!

Morgan DeSimone, BA

Maria Pita, BA

Gary Robinson, LMHC

P.S. Please keep in touch! Let us know how *The Daily Brew Journal* worked for you (or didn't!) so we can make improvements for a subsequent edition!!! Write us at: DailyBrewJournal@gmail.com

P.S.S. Proceeds from the sale of *The Daily Brew Journal* will be used to buy copies for people who can't afford to buy one for themselves.

"Journaling is like whispering to oneself and listening at the same time."

-Mina Murray

Day 1:_____

What 3 things are you most
grateful for in your life right now?

_____

_____

_____

_____

_____

_____

_____

_____

_____

_____

_____

_____

"Real happiness lies in that which never comes nor goes, but simply is."
- Ram Dass

Day 2: _____

Right now my greatest challenge is…

_____

_____

_____

_____

_____

_____

_____

_____

_____

_____

_____

_____

_____

"The strongest people are not those who show strength in front of us,
but those who win battles we know nothing about."
- Jonathan Harnisch

Day 3: _____

What was the last thing that made
you feel deeply frustrated?

_____

_____

_____

_____

_____

_____

_____

_____

_____

_____

_____

_____

_____

_____

_____

"The best way out is always through."
- Robert Frost

Day 4: _____

In conversations, do you tend to listen
or talk more? What are you looking for
when you converse with people?

_____

_____

_____

_____

_____

_____

_____

_____

_____

_____

_____

*"A real conversation always contains an invitation.
You are inviting another person to reveal herself or himself to you,
to tell you who they are or what they want."*
- David Whyte

Day 5: _____

What do you consider a recent failure experience?
What did you learn from the experience?
Is there any way to look at this more positively?

_____

_____

_____

_____

_____

_____

_____

_____

_____

_____

_____

_____

_____

I haven't failed. I've just found 10,000 ways it won't work."
- Thomas Edison

Day 6: _____

What are some positive changes you
can make to your daily routine?

_____

_____

_____

_____

_____

_____

_____

_____

_____

_____

_____

_____

*"I learned to take those experiences that were difficult in my life and
in the adversity that I had overcome to use it for a positive change."*
- Dominique Moceanu

Day 7: _____

Find time today to go outside for a walk in the
most natural place you can find. Observe the
trees, wind, water, etc. Write about how the
experience influences your mood.

_____

_____

_____

_____

_____

_____

_____

_____

_____

_____

"Everything in nature is alive and influences your thoughts whether you know
it or not. Who is to say the rock does not hear your thoughts? Nor the river?
Or the mountain ranges?"
- Tony Ten Fingers (Lakota Sioux)

Day 8: _____

Think back to the person you were
3 years ago. How have you changed?
Has this been a positive or negative change?

_____

_____

_____

_____

_____

_____

_____

_____

_____

_____

_____

"I can't change the direction of the wind, but I can
adjust my sails to always reach my destination."
- Jimmy Dean

Day 9: _____

What makes you feel truly alive?
Can you give examples of such experiences?

_____

_____

_____

_____

_____

_____

_____

_____

_____

_____

_____

_____

_____

_____

"You are the sky. Everything else is just the weather."
- Pema Chodron

Day 10: _____

Below, write a to-do list of the 3 things you'd like to get done in the next couple of days. What will you need to do in order to accomplish these tasks?

_____

_____

_____

_____

_____

_____

_____

_____

_____

_____

_____

_____

"The thing about goals is that living without them is a lot more fun, in the short run. It seems to me, though, that the people who get things done, who lead, who grow and who make an impact... those people have goals."
–Seth Godin

Day 11: _____

What do you need to forgive yourself for?

_____

_____

_____

_____

_____

_____

_____

_____

_____

_____

_____

_____

_____

_____

_____

"Do not give your past the power to define your future."
- Dhiren Prajapati

Day 12: _____

Write about a stressful experience that you encountered in the last year.. Now that it's in the past, do you see it any differently than the day it happened?

_____

_____

_____

_____

_____

_____

_____

_____

_____

_____

"The only thing you sometimes have control over is perspective.
You don't have control over your situation.
But you have a choice about how you view it."
- Chris Pine

Day 13: _____

Write about a difficult time in your life which resulted
in a positive outcome.

_____

_____

_____

_____

_____

_____

_____

_____

_____

_____

_____

_____

"If you change the way you look at things, the things you look at change."
- Wayne Dyer

Day 14: _____

When was the last time you allowed each part of your body to relax? Spend 5 minutes focusing on stretching each part of your body. How does this make you feel afterward? Is stretching an activity you can start incorporating into your daily routine?

_____

_____

_____

_____

_____

_____

_____

_____

_____

_____

_____

"Stretch your mind and fly."
- Whitney Young

Day 15: _____

If you could change anything about yourself, what would it be and why? Is there anything preventing you from making these changes?

_____

_____

_____

_____

_____

_____

_____

_____

_____

_____

_____

_____

"The journey isn't about becoming a different person,
but loving who you are right now."
- Suzanne Heyn

Day 16: _____

What are you most angry about right now
in your life? In what way can you turn this
anger into positive, productive action?

_____

_____

_____

_____

_____

_____

_____

_____

_____

_____

_____

_____

_____

"When angry, count to ten before you speak. If very angry, a hundred."
- Thomas Jefferson

Day 17: _____

Describe your biggest accomplishment in the last year and why it means so much to you.

_____

_____

_____

_____

_____

_____

_____

_____

_____

_____

_____

_____

"It always seems impossible until it's done."
- Nelson Mandela

Day 18: _____

Make it a point to start to read a book today, just for fun. Write down everything you love about the book you're reading. How long did you read for? Does reading something for fun help you relax? Will you continue reading more often?

_____

_____

_____

_____

_____

_____

_____

_____

_____

_____

"A reader lives a thousand lives before he dies...
the man who never reads lives only one."
- George R. R. Martin

Day 19: _____

Describe a time when you sabotaged a good situation for yourself. Explore why you may have done that.

_____

_____

_____

_____

_____

_____

_____

_____

_____

_____

_____

_____

_____

"Our scars do not define us, they remind us where we've been."
- David Rossi

Day 20: _____

How do you define "persistence"? Do you
need to improve your ability to stick with
something, even when the going gets tough?

_____

_____

_____

_____

_____

_____

_____

_____

_____

_____

_____

_____

_____

"When you are going through hell, keep on going. Never, never, never give up."
- Winston Churchill

Day 21: _____

What is an experience that has positively influenced
the way you see yourself or the world around you?
Write about positive decisions you've made, or
believe you will make, as a result of this experience.

_____

_____

_____

_____

_____

_____

_____

_____

_____

_____

_____

"No one else sees the world the way you do, so no
one else can tell the stories that you have to tell."
- Charles de Lint

Day 22: _____

Try to eat a leafy, green vegetable today.
Do you feel healthier? Is this something you
would like to continue doing? Why or why not?

_____

_____

_____

_____

_____

_____

_____

_____

_____

_____

_____

_____

_____

_____

"Health requires healthy food."
- Roger Williams

Day 23: _____

What is a secret you have never shared with anyone before? Why do you think you have kept it a secret?

_____

_____

_____

_____

_____

_____

_____

_____

_____

_____

_____

_____

_____

_____

"Preserve your memories, keep them well. What you forget, you can never retell."
- Louisa May Alcott

Day 24: _____

If I could have any career I would be a/an

_____

because:

_____

_____

_____

_____

_____

_____

_____

_____

_____

_____

_____

"Communication - the human connection -
is the key to personal and career success."
- Paul J. Meyer

Day 25: _____

Describe the childhood memories
which bring you the most joy.

_____

_____

_____

_____

_____

_____

_____

_____

_____

_____

_____

_____

"There is a garden in every childhood, an enchanted place where colors are
brighter, the air softer, and the morning more fragrant than ever again."
- Elizabeth Lawrence

Day 26: _____

In what ways do you treat yourself kindly? How can you show yourself even more affection today?

_____

_____

_____

_____

_____

_____

_____

_____

_____

_____

_____

_____

_____

"Sometimes the most important thing in a whole day
is the rest we take in between two deep breaths."
- Etty Hillesum

Day 27: _____

What does "forgiveness" mean to you?
Who would you like to forgive and what
steps could you take towards forgiveness?

_____

_____

_____

_____

_____

_____

_____

_____

_____

_____

_____

"Until we have seen someone's darkness, we don't really know who they are.
Until we have forgiven someone's darkness, we don't really know what love is."
- Marianne Williamson

Day 28: _____

Go out today and strike up a conversation with a casual acquaintance or a stranger (in a safe, public space). Write about your conversation and how you felt before, during and after. If this was something that could not be done, why?

_____

_____

_____

_____

_____

_____

_____

_____

_____

_____

_____

"If you want something new, you have to stop doing something old."
- Peter F. Drucker

Day 29: _____

Describe a time when you had to make a
really hard decision and what you took
away from this experience afterward.

_____

_____

_____

_____

_____

_____

_____

_____

_____

_____

_____

"Settling for something that does not make you happy
is like diving underwater for air."
- Beau Taplin

Day 30: _____

What do you enjoy doing during your free time?
Explore 3 new activities you might enjoy trying
during your down time this week. Write about them.

_____

_____

_____

_____

_____

_____

_____

_____

_____

_____

_____

_____

_____

"My peronal hobbies are reading, listening to music and silence."
- Edith Sitwell

Day 31: _____

Draw a picture of or write about the biggest obstacle you faced today, and how you overcame this hurdle.

[blank framed box]

"The greater the obstacle, the more glory in overcoming it."
- Moliere

Day 32: _____

What is something you wish others knew about you?
Can you tell someone? Why or why not?

_____

_____

_____

_____

_____

_____

_____

_____

_____

_____

_____

_____

_____

_____

_____

_____

"Blessed are those who can give without remembering and take without forgetting."
- Bernard Meltzer

Day 33: _____

What do you love most about yourself right now?

_____

_____

_____

_____

_____

_____

_____

_____

_____

_____

_____

_____

_____

"Love yourself enough to set boundaries. Your time and energy are precious. You get to choose how you use it. You teach people how to treat you by deciding what you will and won't accept."
- Anna Taylor

Day 34: _____

In what ways are you able to be your own
best friend? Which of these qualities would
you appreciate in someone else?

_____

_____

_____

_____

_____

_____

_____

_____

_____

_____

_____

_____

_____

"Things are never quite as scary when you've got a best friend."
- Bill Watterson

Day 35: _____

Make a list of people you have held or still hold grudges or resentment towards. Describe if you have or have not moved towards forgiveness with each person and what this feels like for you.

_____

_____

_____

_____

_____

_____

_____

_____

_____

_____

_____

_____

"Our greatest freedom is the freedom to choose our attitude."
- Viktor E. Frankl

Day 36: _____

In what ways are you living out-of-alignment
with your values? How can you change this to
live more closely to the things you value?

_____

_____

_____

_____

_____

_____

_____

_____

_____

_____

_____

_____

"When ego is lost, limit is lost. You become infinite, kind, and beautiful."
- Harbhajan Singh Yogi

Day 37: _____

What is holding you back from your dreams?
How can you break free of this?

_____

_____

_____

_____

_____

_____

_____

_____

_____

_____

_____

_____

*"Miracles happen when you give as much
energy to your dreams as you do to your fears."*
- Richard Wilkins

Day 38: _____

There are opportunities around every corner. How can you embrace a new opportunity this week?

_____

_____

_____

_____

_____

_____

_____

_____

_____

_____

_____

_____

"Only those who will risk going too far
can possibly find out how far one can go."
- T. S. Eliot

Day 39: _____

What is a secret someone has shared
with you? How does it make you feel
that they entrusted you with this secret?

_____

_____

_____

_____

_____

_____

_____

_____

_____

_____

_____

_____

"The sun watches what I do, but the moon knows all my secrets."
- J. M. Wonderland

Day 40: _____

What is a dream you've never said out loud?
Have you ever considered writing down this
dream? What might it mean to you?

_____

_____

_____

_____

_____

_____

_____

_____

_____

_____

_____

_____

"A dream doesn't become reality through magic;
it takes sweat, determination and hard work."
- Colin Powell

Day 41: _____

Name 3 moments in your life
when you were ecstatically happy.

_____

_____

_____

_____

_____

_____

_____

_____

_____

_____

_____

"Letting go gives us freedom, and freedom is the only condition
for happiness. If, in our heart, we still cling to anything -
- anger, anxiety, or possessions -- we cannot be free."
- Thich Nhat Hanh

Day 42: _____

In what ways would you like to be able
to expand your own horizons? Are any
of these realistic in the next few months?

_____

_____

_____

_____

_____

_____

_____

_____

_____

_____

_____

_____

_____

"A ship in harbor is safe, but that is not what ships are built for."
- John A. Shedd

Day 43: _____

The 3 things that bother me most right now are...

_____

_____

_____

_____

_____

_____

_____

_____

_____

_____

_____

_____

"Energy is the currency of the universe. When you 'pay' attention to something, you buy that experience. When you allow your consciousness to focus on something that annoys you, you feed it your energy."
- Emily Maroutian

Day 44: _____

What is your philosophy of life? What is the meaning of life for you? What is your purpose? If you don't know or aren't sure, are there things you could do to gain more meaning or purpose in your life?

_____

_____

_____

_____

_____

_____

_____

_____

_____

_____

_____

_____

"Courage doesn't happen when you have all the answers. It happens when you are ready to face the questions you have been avoiding your whole life."
- Shannon L. Alder

Day 45: _____

If you knew this was your last day
on earth what would you do?

_____

_____

_____

_____

_____

_____

_____

_____

_____

_____

_____

_____

_____

_____

"Travel light, live light, spread the light, be the light."
- Yogi Bhajan

The Daily Brew

Day 46: _____

Describe some ways in which
self-reflection has helped you grow?

_____

_____

_____

_____

_____

_____

_____

_____

_____

_____

_____

_____

_____

_____

_____

_____

"Who looks outside, dreams; who looks inside, awakes."
- Carl G. Jung

Day 47: _____

Are you sometimes your own worst enemy? What are some recurring negative thoughts that hold you back? Rewrite these thoughts into positive statements below. Use the next 3 minutes to repeat these positive affirmations to yourself while reflecting on how they make you feel.

_____

_____

_____

_____

_____

_____

_____

_____

_____

"Know that your hopes and dreams have already manifested in the universe and are waiting to impact your life."
- Randi G. Fine

Day 48: _____

Get up early today and watch the sunrise.
Write a poem or photograph the sunrise and
reflect on what you see, hear, smell, and sense.

_____

_____

_____

_____

_____

_____

_____

_____

_____

_____

_____

_____

_____

"The early morning has gold in its mouth."
- Benjamin Franklin

Day 49: _____

Reflect upon what it means to be "the best person you can be." In what ways were you your best self recently? Write about the experience. If you can't think of an example, write about what it would look like if you were your best self.

_____

_____

_____

_____

_____

_____

_____

_____

_____

_____

_____

_____

"I'm competitive with myself. I always try to push past my own borders."
- Tyra Banks

Day 50: _____

What can you do to simplify your life today? This week? This month?

_____

_____

_____

_____

_____

_____

_____

_____

_____

_____

_____

_____

_____

_____

"Our life is frittered away by detail... simplify, simplify."
- Henry David Thoreau

Day 51: _____

Write about the ways in which you might
feel resentment towards yourself or others.
How can you convert that feeling of
resentment into an attitude of forgiveness?

_____

_____

_____

_____

_____

_____

_____

_____

_____

_____

_____

_____

"Anger, resentment and jealousy doesn't change
the heart of others-- it only changes yours."
- Shannon L. Adler

Day 52: _____

Is it more important to be liked by others, or yourself?

_____

_____

_____

_____

_____

_____

_____

_____

_____

_____

_____

_____

_____

_____

"We must be our own before we can be another's."
- Ralph Waldo Emerson

Day 53: _____

What do you wish most people
knew about you and why?

_____

_____

_____

_____

_____

_____

_____

_____

_____

_____

_____

_____

_____

_____

"Do not let the behavior of others destroy your inner peace."
- Dalai Lama XIV

Day 54: _____

What are some healthy ways that you can get rid of some built up stress?

_____

_____

_____

_____

_____

_____

_____

_____

_____

_____

_____

_____

_____

_____

"The best way to find out what we need is to get rid of what we don't."
- Marie Kondo

Day 55: _____

What are the 3 things that worry you the most
and why? In what ways are you able to soothe
your worrying thoughts? Should you use these
approaches more often?

_____

_____

_____

_____

_____

_____

_____

_____

_____

_____

_____

"Be a warrior, not a worrier."
- Unknown

Day 56: _____

Go for a walk today and take in as much
of the natural world as you can. Write
about how nature makes you feel.

_____

_____

_____

_____

_____

_____

_____

_____

_____

_____

_____

_____

_____

"Man's heart, away from nature, becomes hard."
- Luther Standing Bear (Lakota Sioux)

Day 57: _____

Describe the people who make up your
support system. In what ways do these
people help you to be your best self?

_____

_____

_____

_____

_____

_____

_____

_____

_____

_____

_____

_____

"Call it a clan, call it a network, call it a tribe, call it a family.
Whatever you call it, whoever you are, you need one."
- Jane Howard

Day 58: _____

What do you do that makes
you feel healthy or restored?

_____

_____

_____

_____

_____

_____

_____

_____

_____

_____

_____

_____

_____

_____

_____

"A healthy outside starts from the inside."
- Robert Urich

Day 59: _____

Write a letter to someone you hold anger towards.
In the letter include why you are angry with them
and whether or not you forgive them. You can send
it to them if you feel comfortable and safe doing so.
Otherwise, keep it "for your eyes only."

_____

_____

_____

_____

_____

_____

_____

_____

_____

_____

_____

_____

"To forgive is to set a prisoner free and discover that the prisoner was you."
- Lewis B. Smedes

Day 60: _____

Do you consider yourself an introvert or an extrovert?
Or both? Explain.

_____

_____

_____

_____

_____

_____

_____

_____

_____

_____

_____

_____

_____

"When I first read the words 'introvert' and
'extrovert' when I was 10, I thought I was both."
- Annie Dillard

Day 61: _____

Describe a recent time when you felt insecure. What were some thoughts you were having about yourself which may have made it difficult to feel more secure? Have you become more secure in yourself since then? If not, what changes would you have to make to become more secure and confident?

_____

_____

_____

_____

_____

_____

_____

_____

_____

_____

"I am growing flowers in the darkest parts of my heart,
for if light ever enters, it would know where to start."
- Noor Unnahar

Day 62: _____

How do you know when to ask for help? What are some things that you could use a bit of help with right now?

_____

_____

_____

_____

_____

_____

_____

_____

_____

_____

_____

_____

_____

"You get in life what you have the courage to ask for."
- Oprah Winfrey

Day 63: _____

The biggest lessons I've learned
when I've been stressed are....

_____

_____

_____

_____

_____

_____

_____

_____

_____

_____

_____

_____

_____

"For most people, their spiritual teacher is their suffering,
because eventually the suffering brings about awakening."
- Eckhart Tolle

The Daily Do

Day 64: _____

Watch a brief video on-line about someone's experience of spirituality. Does religion or spirituality play a role in your life? Explain.

_____

_____

_____

_____

_____

_____

_____

_____

_____

_____

_____

"Happiness cannot be traveled to, owned, earned, worn or consumed. Happiness is the spiritual experience of living every minute with love, grace, and gratitude."
- Denis Waitley

Day 65: _____

Describe some ways you are confident and some ways you aren't as confident. Can anything be learned from this comparison?

_____

_____

_____

_____

_____

_____

_____

_____

_____

_____

_____

"With the realization of one's own potential and
self-confidence in one's ability, one can build a better world."
- Dalai Lama XIV

Day 66: _____

Observe how you have expressed your
feelings throughout the day. In retrospect,
how could you have expressed your feelings
differently to produce a different outcome?

_____

_____

_____

_____

_____

_____

_____

_____

_____

_____

_____

_____

*"The more room you give yourself to express your true thoughts and
feelings, the more room there is for your wisdom to emerge."*
- Marianne Williamson

Day 67: _____

Yell into or punch a pillow or mattress. Let out all
your anger, sadness, and frustrations. Write about
what caused you to feel this way and how you felt
after experiencing this release.

_____

_____

_____

_____

_____

_____

_____

_____

_____

_____

_____

"Let today be the day you finally release yourself from the
imprisonment of past grudges and anger. Simplify your life. Let go
of the poisonous past and live abundantly the beautiful present... today."
- Dr. Steve Maraboli

Day 68: _____

Where does your mind live the most: in the past, present, or future? Describe how your mind gravitates to one or the other and why. What are the benefits of living in the present moment?

_____

_____

_____

_____

_____

_____

_____

_____

_____

_____

_____

_____

"Yesterday is history, tomorrow is a mystery, today is a gift,
that's why we call it the 'present.'"
- Alice Morse Earle

Day 69: _____

Have you ever run away from home? Did you
ever want to? Describe your feelings about
wanting, or not wanting, to leave home?

_____

_____

_____

_____

_____

_____

_____

_____

_____

_____

_____

"My heart swings back and forth between the
need for routine and the urge to run."
- Unknown

Day 70: _____

What experiences and resources do you need to better yourself? Are any of these experiences or resources close at hand? If not, what will it take to make them more accessible?

_____

_____

_____

_____

_____

_____

_____

_____

_____

_____

_____

_____

"Some days I am the flower, some days I am the rain."
- Pavana

Day 71: _____

What was a recent embarrassing
moment and why? In hindsight, how
can you view that moment differently?

_____

_____

_____

_____

_____

_____

_____

_____

_____

_____

_____

_____

_____

"The real difficulty is to overcome how you think about yourself."
- Maya Angelou

Day 72: _____

Think of a person you care about who is going through a difficult time. Close your eyes and visualize for 3 minutes what it would feel like to walk in their shoes. Write about the experience and your feelings.

_____

_____

_____

_____

_____

_____

_____

_____

_____

_____

_____

"It is under the greatest adversity that there exists the greatest potential for doing good, both for oneself and others."
- Dalai Lama XIV

Day 73: _____

Describe your perfect relationship.

_____

_____

_____

_____

_____

_____

_____

_____

_____

_____

_____

_____

_____

_____

"If you wish to be a warrior, prepare to get broken. If you wish to be an explorer, prepare to get lost. And if you wish to be a lover, prepare to be both."
- Daniel Saint

Day 74: _____

On a scale of 1-10 my mental health is at a

_____

because...

_____

_____

_____

_____

_____

_____

_____

_____

_____

_____

"It was when I stopped searching for home within others and lifted the foundations of home within myself, I found there were roots more intimate than those between a mind and body that have decided to be whole."
- Rupi Kaur

Day 75: _____

Name a frustration you have right now.
How can you release yourself of this?

_____

_____

_____

_____

_____

_____

_____

_____

_____

_____

_____

_____

"Like a sandcastle, all is temporary. Build it, tend it,
enjoy it, and when the time comes, let it go."
- Jack Kornfield

Day 76: _____

Think of ways you can touch someone's life
through small gestures. Make one gesture
today and reflect on how this made you feel.

_____

_____

_____

_____

_____

_____

_____

_____

_____

_____

_____

*"Whatever you choose for yourself, give to another. If you
choose to be happy, cause another to be happy. If you choose
to be prosperous, cause another to prosper. If you choose more
love in your life, cause another to have more love in theirs."*
- Neale Donald Walsch

Day 77: _____

What would you do if you weren't afraid of failing?

_____

_____

_____

_____

_____

_____

_____

_____

_____

_____

_____

_____

_____

"And the day came that the risk it took to remain tight in the
bud became more painful than the risk it took to blossom."
- Anais Nin

Day 78: _____

What is an experience from your childhood that, while difficult at the time, has proved to be valuable?

_____

_____

_____

_____

_____

_____

_____

_____

_____

_____

_____

_____

_____

"Strength doesn't come from what you can do. It comes from overcoming the things you once thought you couldn't."
- Rikki Rogers

Day 79: _____

What expectations do you feel from your family or society? Evaluate these expectations and write about which ones will help you achieve your goals and which ones no longer serve you.

_____

_____

_____

_____

_____

_____

_____

_____

_____

_____

_____

_____

"When you release yourself of expectations, you are free to enjoy things for what they are instead of what you think they should be"
- Mandy Hale

Day 80: _____

Who is the person who you tell the most things to?
How did you build this level of trust in this person?

_____

_____

_____

_____

_____

_____

_____

_____

_____

_____

_____

_____

_____

_____

"One of the most beautiful qualities of true
friendship is to understand and to be understood."
- Lucius Annaeus Seneca

Day 81: _____

Recall a successful experience you've had recently.
What has it taught you about your ability to succeed?
What can you do to celebrate your accomplishments?

_____

_____

_____

_____

_____

_____

_____

_____

_____

_____

*"I cannot give you the formula for success, but I can give you
the formula for failure—which is to try and please everybody."*
- H.B. Swope

Day 82: _____

Today, do your best to actively listen during a conversation with a friend. Challenge yourself to only do about 20% of the talking while your friend does about 80%. How did the conversation go? How can you become a better listener?

_____

_____

_____

_____

_____

_____

_____

_____

_____

_____

_____

_____

"The quieter you become, the more you can hear."
- Ram Dass

Day 83: _____

Reflect back on the last argument you had with someone. Now, try putting yourself in their shoes. How does this make you feel? Do you feel any differently now than you did initially?

_____

_____

_____

_____

_____

_____

_____

_____

_____

_____

_____

_____

"The aim of argument, or discussion, should not be victory, but progress."
- Joseph Joubert

The Daily Brew

Day 84: _____

What's your favorite book and why? What about this book do you like so much? Why does it speak to you?

_____

_____

_____

_____

_____

_____

_____

_____

_____

_____

_____

"The MORE that you READ, the more
THINGS you will KNOW. The MORE you
LEARN, the more PLACES you'll GO!"
- Dr. Seuss

Day 85: _____

Which part of your personality are you
least likely to share with other people?

_____

_____

_____

_____

_____

_____

_____

_____

_____

_____

_____

_____

"The deepest pain I ever felt was denying my
own feelings to make others feel comfortable."
-Nicole Lyons

Day 86: _____

Give examples of opportunities where you could have accepted help in your life and opportunities where you did accept help. What does it mean to you to accept help?

_____

_____

_____

_____

_____

_____

_____

_____

_____

_____

_____

_____

"A candle loses nothing by lighting another candle."
- James Keller

Day 87: _____

Many people feel uneasy during transition periods.
How do you feel about change?

_____

_____

_____

_____

_____

_____

_____

_____

_____

_____

_____

_____

_____

_____

"You are allowed to be a masterpiece and a work in progress, simultaneously."
- Sophia Bush

Day 88: _____

Consider what you have accomplished in the
last week. In what ways were you successful?
In what ways can you be more productive?

_____

_____

_____

_____

_____

_____

_____

_____

_____

_____

_____

_____

_____

_____

"In order to love yourself, you cannot hate the experiences that have shaped you."
- Andrea Dykstra

Day 89: _____

Identify one thing you've always wished for. In what ways can you come closer to granting your own wish?

_____

_____

_____

_____

_____

_____

_____

_____

_____

_____

_____

_____

_____

_____

"Every accomplishment starts with a decision to try."
- Gail Devers

Day 90: _____

In what ways do you find it difficult to take
responsibility for your actions? Why might this
be a challenging task? What can you do to help
in the act of self-accountability?

_____

_____

_____

_____

_____

_____

_____

_____

_____

_____

"Nothing others do is because of you. What others say and do is a projection
of their own reality, their own dream. When you are immune to the opinions and
actions of others, you won't be the victim of needless suffering."
- Don Miguel Ruiz

Day 91: _____

List some beliefs that are different from your own.
How do you handle a situation in which a person's
beliefs are significantly different from your own?

_____

_____

_____

_____

_____

_____

_____

_____

_____

_____

_____

"Our core beliefs are at the very center of who we are, what we believe about
ourselves, what we think about others, and how we feel about life as a whole."
- Aletheia Luna

Day 92: _____

Many people of Hindu and Buddhist faiths believe that the mandala, exemplified below, is a symbol of completeness and self-unity. As you color, trace, or simply look at this mandala, reflect on what makes you feel complete or unified.

"He who experiences the unity of life sees his own self in all beings, and all beings in his own self, and looks on everything with an impartial eye."
- Buddha

Day 93: _____

Express your 3 biggest fears and how you are able to navigate them. How can you change negative thinking about your fears into positive thoughts?

_____

_____

_____

_____

_____

_____

_____

_____

_____

_____

_____

"You can conquer almost any fear if you will only make up your mind to do so. For remember, fear doesn't exist anywhere except in the mind."
- Dale Carnegie

The Daily Brew

Day 94: _____

No matter how terrible my day is, these
3 things can always make me feel better:

_____

_____

_____

_____

_____

_____

_____

_____

_____

_____

_____

"Every now and then go away, have a little relaxation, for when you come back to your work your judgment will be surer. Go some distance away because then the work appears smaller and more of it can be taken in at a glance and a lack of harmony and proportion is more readily seen."
- Leonardo da Vinci

Day 95: _____

Do you prefer organized chaos or structured routines? How does this preference assist in the everyday functioning of your mind, body, and spirit?

_____

_____

_____

_____

_____

_____

_____

_____

_____

_____

_____

"And that is all she ever wanted. For everyone around her to embrace their storms and make them fall in love with their own violent winds."
- R. M. Drake

Day 96: _____

Identify a plan you have for the future. This can be something you wish to accomplish, a destination you would like to travel to, or even a layout of the upcoming week! Write about the options you have to help you achieve this goal.

_____

_____

_____

_____

_____

_____

_____

_____

_____

_____

_____

_____

"The best way to predict your future is to create it."
- Abraham Lincoln

Day 97: _____

What encourages you to be your best self?

_____

_____

_____

_____

_____

_____

_____

_____

_____

_____

_____

_____

_____

_____

_____

"The inspiration you seek is already within you. Be silent and listen."
- Rumi

Day 98: _____

If you were asked to write a thank you letter
to your body, what would you say? How does
your body support you each day?

_____

_____

_____

_____

_____

_____

_____

_____

_____

_____

_____

_____

*"And I said to my body softly, 'I want to be your friend.' It took a long
breath and replied, 'I have been waiting my whole life for this."*
- Nayyirah Waheed

Day 99: _____

Have you ever felt reluctant to tell someone your thoughts? Were you able to ultimately say what was on your mind? How did you do so?

_____

_____

_____

_____

_____

_____

_____

_____

_____

_____

_____

"Once you replace negative thoughts with positive ones,
you'll start having positive results."
- Willie Nelson

Day 100: _____

After 99 days of self-reflection, what have you learned about yourself? How have you experienced change? Which limiting beliefs are gone, and which are still present?

_____

_____

_____

_____

_____

_____

_____

_____

_____

_____

_____

_____

"Learning without reflection is a waste. Reflection without learning is dangerous."
- Confucius

Day 101: _____

What's something that was constantly on your mind as a child? Is there any connection to you in the present day?

_____

_____

_____

_____

_____

_____

_____

_____

_____

_____

_____

"Today's a perfect day for a whole new start.
Let go of fear and free your mind. It's time to open your heart."
- Chris Butler

Day 102: _____

In what ways do you compare yourself to others? Is comparing yourself a positive or negative tendency? What advice would you give yourself about this behavior?

_____

_____

_____

_____

_____

_____

_____

_____

_____

_____

_____

_____

"A flower does not think of competing to the flower next to it, it just blooms."
- Zen Shin

Day 103: _____

Name 3 things you can start doing
to take better care of yourself.

_____

_____

_____

_____

_____

_____

_____

_____

_____

_____

_____

_____

_____

_____

_____

"To love oneself is the beginning of a lifelong romance."
- Oscar Wilde

Day 104: _____

In what ways do your suggestions and comments affect people in your life? How could you present your ideas so that they would have more positive impact on others?

_____

_____

_____

_____

_____

_____

_____

_____

_____

_____

_____

_____

"There is a voice that doesn't use words. Listen."
- Rumi

Day 105: _____

What's something about yourself that you aren't always honest with yourself or others about? Explain. What would be the pros and cons of becoming more honest about this issue?

_____

_____

_____

_____

_____

_____

_____

_____

_____

_____

_____

"Honesty is the first chapter in the book of wisdom."
- Thomas Jefferson

Day 106: _____

A silver lining in a not-so-good
situation that recently happened is...

_____

_____

_____

_____

_____

_____

_____

_____

_____

_____

_____

_____

*"I've learned that no matter what happens, or how bad it
seems today, life goes on, and it will be better tomorrow."*
- Maya Angelou

Day 107: _____

Write a letter to your past self. What would have soothed or comforted you at that time? What advice would you have given yourself? Offer your past self the acceptance and love that you needed.

_____

_____

_____

_____

_____

_____

_____

_____

_____

_____

_____

_____

"Write hard and clear about what hurts."
- Ernest Hemingway

Day 108: _____

What was the biggest mistake you made this week?
Have you been too hard on yourself about this
choice? How can you change your thinking about it to
help you in the future?

_____

_____

_____

_____

_____

_____

_____

_____

_____

_____

_____

_____

"You will only fail to learn, if you do not learn from failing."
- Stella Adler

Day 109: _____

Try to find and circle all of the words listed below. Some are frontwards, some are backwards, some are diagonal. Do your best but don't stress if you can't find them all today. You can always come back and try again another day!

```
G E N A N G V T H S T N P Q Y Z Z Y S F
N N S D F T N K Y T I V I T A E R C S E
I F L S X F Q I J Y O R I A S Q U O E E
L E Y P B I I F T Y J L W N Y U V F N L
A I Y I W E R R L P A P O S I T I V E I
E L N H Y I H I M N E I G N I V I G R N
H E X S E R M A O A T C K M G V T G A G
R B R N I A E S V O T F C I K X A G W S
A Y D O F G R V M I J I L A M H C C A B
X S T I D E H E O O O I O O I B H O B U
Z E P T P V G T U C F R T N J P I U A P
A M Z A B S G R F E E H X A D P E R D K
X P E L D D N L V E O R N H T J V A F P
P O W E R A U E D U T I T T A Y E G C A
D S F R L F O R G I V E N E S S M E H E
E D K I P Q R H J N A F P O M T E M Q I
L G N L E T T I I X A Q S L K J N L Z V
T G E P Q S R D D M Z H R O J I T D N D
L H B E N E F I T R L B C V W C E B O F
Q I V M U G G U G V Q J S E H F A B V G
```

ACCEPTING	FORGIVENESS
ACHIEVEMENT	GIVING
AFFIRMATION	HEALING
ATTITUDE	HELPFUL
AWARENESS	INSIGHT
BEHAVIOR	JOURNALING
BELIEF	LIFE
BENEFIT	LOVE
CHANGE	RECOVERY
COURAGE	RELATIONSHIPS
CREATIVITY	PEACE
EMOTIONS	PERSONALITY
FAMILY	POSITIVE
FEELINGS	POWER
FRIENDS	THOUGHTS

Day 110: _____

How is the way you see yourself different from
the ways in which someone might see you?

_____

_____

_____

_____

_____

_____

_____

_____

_____

_____

_____

_____

_____

_____

_____

_____

"How you love yourself is how you teach others to love you."
- Rupi Kaur

Day 111: _____

What can you do today to
improve your mental health?

_____

_____

_____

_____

_____

_____

_____

_____

_____

_____

_____

_____

"Train your mind to see the good in everything. Positivity is a choice.
The happiness of your life depends on the quality of your thoughts."
- Dr. Bilal Philips

Day 112: _____

In what ways might you be standing in
your own way? How can you change this?

_____

_____

_____

_____

_____

_____

_____

_____

_____

_____

_____

_____

*"You don't have to have it all figured
out to move forward, just take the next step."*
- Melanie Beckler

Day 113: _____

What is your view on family? Who do you consider to be in your own immediate family? Are there any non-relatives who you might consider to be equally as important as a family member?

_____

_____

_____

_____

_____

_____

_____

_____

_____

_____

_____

_____

"In family life, love is the oil that eases friction, the cement that binds closer together, and the music that brings harmony."
- Friedrich Nietzsche

Day 114: _____

What is your definition of "love"? Who makes you feel loved, and what qualities do they have that create loving feelings in you?

_____

_____

_____

_____

_____

_____

_____

_____

_____

_____

_____

"She doesn't want to hear that she is flawless, she wants to hear that she is loved, regardless of the flaws."
- Charming Winds

Day 115: _____

When times get tough, what is most important for you to remind yourself? Make today an opportunity to write about a difficult time when you had to utilize this skill.

_____

_____

_____

_____

_____

_____

_____

_____

_____

_____

_____

"Every day is a new beginning. Take a deep breath and start again."
- Unknown

Day 116: _____

Describe the ways in which you manage your anger.
Give examples of ways you can communicate your
frustration before it reaches the anger stage.

_____

_____

_____

_____

_____

_____

_____

_____

_____

_____

_____

_____

_____

"You will not be punished for your anger, you will be punished by your anger."
- Buddha

Day 117: _____

Seek out a funny movie, video, etc. and have a good "belly laugh". How did this make you feel?

_____

_____

_____

_____

_____

_____

_____

_____

_____

_____

_____

_____

_____

"The most wasted day of all is that in which we have not laughed."
- Sebastion-Roch Nicolas Chamfort

Day 118: _____

In what ways has your life taken unexpected turns?
What does this tell you about planning and control?

_____

_____

_____

_____

_____

_____

_____

_____

_____

_____

_____

_____

"Our anxiety does not come from thinking about
the future, but from wanting to control it."
- Kahlil Gibran

Day 119: _____

What do you need most in order to heal?

_____

_____

_____

_____

_____

_____

_____

_____

_____

_____

_____

_____

"Free yourself from the illusion of a good and bad day.
Labeling times makes us nostalgic of the past and demanding
of the future. There is only here and now, let it be."
- Ram Dass

Day 120: _____

Who is your biggest critic? Explain how this person affects you in positive or negative ways.

_____

_____

_____

_____

_____

_____

_____

_____

_____

_____

_____

_____

_____

_____

"No one can make you feel inferior without your consent."
- Eleanor Roosevelt

Day 121: _____

Think of a good friend. What are their best characteristics? Why do you like these characteristics?

_____

_____

_____

_____

_____

_____

_____

_____

_____

_____

_____

_____

_____

"A friend is someone who helps you up when you're down,
and if they can't, they lay down beside you and listen."
- Winnie the Pooh

The Daily Brew

Day 122: _____

Who is your hero and why?

_____

_____

_____

_____

_____

_____

_____

_____

_____

_____

_____

_____

_____

_____

_____

"A hero is someone who understands the
responsibility that comes with his freedom."
- Bob Dylan

Day 123: _____

What makes you feel nourished
on all levels (mind, body and spirit)?

_____

_____

_____

_____

_____

_____

_____

_____

_____

_____

_____

"The mind is like water. When it's turbulent, it's difficult to see.
When it's calm, everything becomes clear."
- Prasad Mahes

Day 124: _____

How has life been unfair to you? How can you view
these experiences without feeling like the victim?

_____

_____

_____

_____

_____

_____

_____

_____

_____

_____

_____

_____

"Sometimes you just need to talk about something - not to get sympathy or help,
but just to kill its power by allowing the truth to hit the air."
- Karen Salmansohn

Day 125: _____

How do you want to be remembered in life?

_____

_____

_____

_____

_____

_____

_____

_____

_____

_____

_____

_____

_____

_____

"I would like to be remembered as a person who wanted to be free...
so other people would be also free."
- Rosa Parks

Day 126: _____

In what ways do you feel limited?
How can you emancipate yourself from this?

_____

_____

_____

_____

_____

_____

_____

_____

_____

_____

_____

_____

_____

_____

"Rule your mind or it will rule you."
- Buddha

Day 127: _____

What does connecting with nature mean to you?
Make a plan to do this during the upcoming week.

_____

_____

_____

_____

_____

_____

_____

_____

_____

_____

_____

_____

_____

_____

"Look deep into nature, and then you will understand everything better."
- Albert Einstein

Day 128: _____

What is the best trip you've gone on? Who did you go with? Is there anything you learned during this trip?

_____

_____

_____

_____

_____

_____

_____

_____

_____

_____

_____

_____

_____

_____

"If we were meant to stay in one place, we'd have roots instead of feet, he said."
- Rachel Wolchin

Day 129: _____

What are you looking forward to the most this year?

_____

_____

_____

_____

_____

_____

_____

_____

_____

_____

_____

_____

"Life will only change when you become more committed
to your dreams than you are to your comfort zone."
- Billy Cox

Day 130: _____

What was the best compliment you ever received? Why? Write about your feelings associated with compliments.

_____

_____

_____

_____

_____

_____

_____

_____

_____

_____

_____

_____

_____

"....You owe yourself the love that you so freely give to other people."
- Alexandra Elle

The Daily Do

Day 131: _____

Sit back, relax, close your eyes, and take 3 minutes to connect with your inner peace. Reflect upon how you feel afterwards.

_____

_____

_____

_____

_____

_____

_____

_____

_____

_____

_____

_____

_____

"Your sacred space is where you can find yourself over and over again."
- Joseph Campbell

Day 132: _____

What annoys you most about people? How can you view them differently so you are less annoyed?

_____

_____

_____

_____

_____

_____

_____

_____

_____

_____

_____

_____

_____

"Anyone who has declared someone else to be an idiot, a bad apple,
is annoyed when it turns out in the end that he isn't."
- Friedrich Nietzsche

$\mathcal{D}$ay 133: _____

What piece of advice would you
give to your five year old self?

_____

_____

_____

_____

_____

_____

_____

_____

_____

_____

_____

_____

_____

"There is always one moment in childhood
where the door opens and lets the future in. "
- Graham Greene

Day 134: _____

Spend time today with your or a friend's pet or ask a stranger if you can pet their dog. Write about how being in the presence of animals makes you feel.

_____

_____

_____

_____

_____

_____

_____

_____

_____

_____

_____

"Animals are such agreeable friends--they
ask no questions, they pass no criticisms."
- George Elliott

Day 135: _____

Reflect upon any nervous habits you
might have. How can you reinvent these
habits into positive behaviors?

_____

_____

_____

_____

_____

_____

_____

_____

_____

_____

_____

_____

"Between stimulus and response there's a space, in that space lies our power to
choose our response, in our response lies our growth and our freedom."
- Viktor Frankl

Day 136: _____

When you're alone, what makes you feel safe?
Describe some positive aspects of your safe spaces.

_____

_____

_____

_____

_____

_____

_____

_____

_____

_____

_____

"The one thing you have that nobody else has is you.
Your voice, your mind, your story, your vision. So write and draw
and build and play and dance and live as only you can."
- Neil Gaiman

Day 137: _____

What is a trait that you admire most in others?
In what ways do you see that trait in yourself?

_____

_____

_____

_____

_____

_____

_____

_____

_____

_____

_____

_____

*"The more I think about it, the more I realize
there is nothing more artistic than to love others."*
- Vincent Van Gogh

Day 138: _____

What is one thing that can always
put the pep in your step?

_____

_____

_____

_____

_____

_____

_____

_____

_____

_____

_____

_____

_____

_____

"Respond to every call that excites your spirit."
- Rumi

Day 139: _____

What character traits do you
feel need to be improved?

_____

_____

_____

_____

_____

_____

_____

_____

_____

_____

"I can tell you character traits I admire and work to develop in myself -
perseverance, self-discipline, courage to stand up for what is right even when it is
against one's friends or one's self."
- Dalia Mogahed

Day 140: _____

What is something you would like to learn how to do? Why? How can you learn to do this? Will you make it a point to begin learning this activity?

_____

_____

_____

_____

_____

_____

_____

_____

_____

_____

_____

"Success is no accident. It is hard work, perseverance, learning, studying, sacrifice and most of all, love of what you are doing or learning to do."
- Pele

Day 141: _____

Color this Mandala and observe
your creative thoughts as you go.

Write your own inspirational quote to
reflect your Mandala experience.

Day 142: _____

Have you learned any lessons from love?
What has it taught you? Are you more
protective or more trusting as a result?

_____

_____

_____

_____

_____

_____

_____

_____

_____

_____

_____

_____

_____

"Sometimes the heart sees what is invisible to the eye."
- H. Jackson Brown, Jr.

Day 143: _____

What are some things that help you deal with hard times? Create a list and write about how each one helps you.

_____

_____

_____

_____

_____

_____

_____

_____

_____

_____

_____

_____

_____

"If it comes, let it come. If it stays, let it stay. If it goes, let it go."
- Nicholas Sparks

Day 144: _____

Do you choose to think your thoughts,
or do your thoughts choose you?

_____

_____

_____

_____

_____

_____

_____

_____

_____

_____

_____

_____

_____

_____

_____

"What we think, we become."
- Buddha

Day 145: _____

What does "unconditional love" mean to you?
Think of a way you can give unconditional
love to someone you know and trust today
and write about your experience.

_____

_____

_____

_____

_____

_____

_____

_____

_____

_____

_____

"The greatest gift that you can give to others
is the gift of unconditional love and acceptance."
- Brian Tracy

Day 146: _____

What is your all-time favorite memory? Recall each of your senses from this particular memory.

_____

_____

_____

_____

_____

_____

_____

_____

_____

_____

_____

*"Sometimes you will never know the value
of a moment until it becomes a memory."*
- Dr. Seuss

Day 147: _____

How would you describe the current state of your physical health and wellbeing? Is your health within your own control? If any of these aspects are out of your control, how can you find acceptance over the state of your health?

_____

_____

_____

_____

_____

_____

_____

_____

_____

_____

"A calm mind brings inner strength and self-confidence, so that's very important for good health."
- Dalai Lama XIV

Day 148: _____

Write about a time when you experienced an unhealthy relationship. Identify any red flags that you recall and what information you would have been interested in knowing about the person in the introduction stage.

_____

_____

_____

_____

_____

_____

_____

_____

_____

_____

_____

_____

"If they do it often, it isn't a mistake, it's just their behavior."
- Dr. Steve Maraboli

Day 149: _____

What is the best advice you have
ever given to someone? To yourself?

_____

_____

_____

_____

_____

_____

_____

_____

_____

_____

_____

_____

"To be yourself in a world that is constantly trying to
make you something else is the greatest accomplishment."
- Ralph Waldo Emerson

Day 150: _____

Describe a time or situation when you
felt out of control and how that made you
feel. Upon reflection, what can you do
now to feel more in control of the event?

_____

_____

_____

_____

_____

_____

_____

_____

_____

_____

_____

_____

*"Inner peace begins the moment you choose not to allow
another person or event to control your emotions."*
- Pema Chodron

Day 151: _____

Read a current headline news story online or in a newspaper. Summarize what you read. Was this story positive or negative? How does this make you feel? Are you over-exposed or under-exposed to things going on in the world?

_____

_____

_____

_____

_____

_____

_____

_____

_____

"Everyone has inside of him a piece of good news. The good news is that you don't know how great you can be! How much you can love! What you can accomplish! And what your potential is!"
- Anne Frank

Day 152: _____

Who is the first person you call when you're in trouble? And why? What are the most important qualities of being there for others?

_____

_____

_____

_____

_____

_____

_____

_____

_____

_____

_____

"Where would you be without friends? The people to pick you up when you need lifting? We come from homes far from perfect, so you end up almost parent and sibling to your friends - your own chosen family. There's nothing like a really loyal, dependable, good friend. Nothing."
- Jennifer Aniston

Day 153: _____

How many of your current friendships have lasted more than two years? Which of these people do you feel will still be important to you ten years from now? Why or why not?

_____

_____

_____

_____

_____

_____

_____

_____

_____

_____

_____

_____

"A friend is one that knows you as you are, understands where you have been, accepts what you have become, and still gently allows you to grow."
- William Shakespeare

Day 154: _____

Do you think you're brave? Think of an
example when you demonstrated bravery.

_____

_____

_____

_____

_____

_____

_____

_____

_____

_____

_____

_____

_____

"Loyalty and devotion lead to bravery. Bravery leads to the spirit of self-sacrifice. The spirit of self-sacrifice creates trust in the power of love."
- Morihei Ueshiba

Day 155: _____

In what ways can you incorporate exercise into your routine today? How do you feel about physical activity?

_____

_____

_____

_____

_____

_____

_____

_____

_____

_____

_____

_____

_____

"Your body is your most priceless possession. Take care of it."
- Jack LaLanne

Day 156: _____

Make a 3 item list of things that make you happy, and 3 things that make you upset. Can you use the 3 things that make you happy to overcome the 3 things that make you upset?

_____

_____

_____

_____

_____

_____

_____

_____

_____

_____

_____

_____

"The goal is not to get rid of all your negative thoughts and feelings; that's impossible. The goal is to change your response to them."
- Unknown

Day 157: _____

Is guilt a feeling given to us by others, or one we place upon ourselves? How can you relinquish yourself from any feelings of guilt?

_____

_____

_____

_____

_____

_____

_____

_____

_____

_____

_____

_____

"Sometimes you get the best light from a burning bridge."
- Don Henley

Day 158: _____

What's something you regret doing or not doing recently? If you could turn back time, is there anything you would do differently? Why or why not?

_____

_____

_____

_____

_____

_____

_____

_____

_____

_____

_____

_____

"When one door closes, another opens; but we often look so long and so regretfully upon the closed door that we do not see the one which has opened for us."
- Alexander Graham Bell

Day 159: _____

What is the most inspiring thing someone has ever said to you? How has this changed the way you do/see things?

_____

_____

_____

_____

_____

_____

_____

_____

_____

_____

_____

"Change will not happen if we wait for some other person or some other time. We are the ones we've been waiting for. We are the change that we seek."
- Barack Obama

The Daily Do

Day 160: _____

Go on a nature walk. Become aware of all the
different sounds you hear. Was this relaxing?
What did you reflect upon during your walk?

_____

_____

_____

_____

_____

_____

_____

_____

_____

_____

_____

_____

"In every walk with nature one receives far more than he seeks."
- John Muir

Day 161: _____

What is something or who is someone
you love unconditionally? Explain.

_____

_____

_____

_____

_____

_____

_____

_____

_____

_____

_____

_____

*"I think in a lot of ways unconditional love is a myth.
My mom's the only reason I know it's the real thing."*
- Conor Oberst

Day 162: _____

What are your most destructive habits?
What are a few things you could do to
work on breaking these habits?

_____

_____

_____

_____

_____

_____

_____

_____

_____

_____

_____

_____

_____

"Chains of habit are too light to be felt until they are too heavy to be broken."
- Warren Buffet

Day 163: _____

What are your feelings about time?
Do you have enough of it? Why or why not?

_____

_____

_____

_____

_____

_____

_____

_____

_____

_____

_____

_____

_____

_____

_____

"The price of anything is the amount of life you spend on it."
- Henry David Thoreau

Day 164: _____

When was the last time you ate? Describe your
relationship with food. Is there any way to
make this relationship healthier?

_____

_____

_____

_____

_____

_____

_____

_____

_____

_____

_____

_____

"To eat is a necessity, but to eat intelligently is an art."
- François de la Rochefoucauld

Day 165: _____

What/who is your motivation and why?

_____

_____

_____

_____

_____

_____

_____

_____

_____

_____

_____

_____

_____

_____

"What you get by achieving your goals is not as important as what you become by achieving your goals."
- Zig Ziglar

Day 166: _____

What might be helpful to you right now? What makes you more apt to help others? Should you focus more on helping yourself or helping others? Explain.

_____

_____

_____

_____

_____

_____

_____

_____

_____

_____

_____

"The purpose of human life is to serve, and to show compassion and the will to help others."
- Albert Schweitzer

The Daily Do

Day 167: _____

Call or e-mail someone who has made a significant impact in your life, and thank them. If you can no longer get in contact with this person, write them a letter below to express your feelings of gratitude. How did this phone call, letter or e-mail make you feel?

_____

_____

_____

_____

_____

_____

_____

_____

_____

_____

*"The single biggest problem with communication
is the illusion that it has taken place."*
- George Bernard Shaw

Day 168: _____

How has a trauma or significant issue influenced
other aspects of your life: family, work, personal
relationships, living situation and so on? In what
ways have you changed as a result of this trauma/
issue? Is this something for which you received
help or should seek help?

_____

_____

_____

_____

_____

_____

_____

_____

_____

*"The paradox of trauma is that it has both the power
to destroy and the power to transform and resurrect."*
- Peter A. Levine

Day 169: _____

What is something you strongly believe in? How does this belief influence your choices and behaviors?

_____

_____

_____

_____

_____

_____

_____

_____

_____

_____

_____

_____

"If you believe it will work out, you'll see opportunities.
If you believe it won't, you will see obstacles."
- Wayne Dyer

Day 170: _____

As explained in the beginning of this journal, the occasional hot beverage can offer tremendous impacts to both your physical and mental health. Try to find and circle all of the "hot beverage" words listed below. Some are frontwards, some are backwards, some are diagonal. Maybe even grab a warm drink to sip on while you do this!

```
B O B L A C K T E A H J N J V J T G D F
Z L S W A T S C E S I B A A P D Z P U R
S G A S I K W G I G C V N Q M U C L Q E
O U W C E G A R F N A I Z C E R C C Q S
N M A J K R I Y B O L R P E E F F O C H
E V I R E C P B M L C J N O I A E T P J
E Z U V O X O S A O M V V C U F N A K B
R M E A J M S F E O D P E H J R J L D T
G B P T L N A X F K Z D E C A F I A A C
O F O Y E A I N O E C G T O N F L N D R
K B T Y C V B J D O E W C Z P Y U L G E
M Q S W A T E R F N A E B E E F F O C A
I A F J P Y M F E P X G C N B G K T X M
L G Y F P W E L H H P V U S Y Q N W E E
K K S R U E B H Q F E R W B B E I I P R
Y G G O C G T Z H L G E M E N Y R L D C
F A M E C U C T T O E R A G U S D F K B
K Y M L I B F T A T N G K H B J T O R P
U F I H N X E N P L A E P E T Q O U R E
U D L S O K X X X C M H Y Y Y M H T I I
```

AROMA	HOT DRINK
BEVERAGE	ICED COFFEE
BLACK COFFEE	IRISH
BLACK TEA	JAVA
CAPPUCCINO	KETTLE
COFFEE	LATTE
COFFEE BEAN	MILK
CREAMER	MUG
CUP	OOLONG
DECAF	POURING
ESPRESSO	SUGAR
FRESH	SWEET
GREEN	TEA
HERBAL	VANILLA
HONEY	WATER

Day 171: _____

How would one of your good friends describe you?

_____

_____

_____

_____

_____

_____

_____

_____

_____

_____

_____

_____

_____

_____

_____

"A faithful friend is the medicine of life."
- Ecclesiasties 6:16

Day 172: _____

What is your favorite way to spend the day?

_____

_____

_____

_____

_____

_____

_____

_____

_____

_____

_____

_____

_____

"There are only two ways to live your life. One is as though
nothing is a miracle. The other is as though everything is."
- Albert Einstein

Day 173: _____

What qualities do you admire in others? Do you see
any of these qualities within yourself as well?

_____

_____

_____

_____

_____

_____

_____

_____

_____

_____

_____

_____

_____

_____

"Go easy on yourself. Whatever you do today, let it be enough."
- Unknown

Day 174: _____

Imagine something that makes you smile and make
an intention to smile at others today as you think of
this thought. What kind of reactions did you get from
the other people and how did this make you feel?

_____

_____

_____

_____

_____

_____

_____

_____

_____

_____

_____

"You are not a drop in the ocean. You are the entire ocean in a drop"
- Rumi

Day 175: _____

If you could change anything about your upbringing, what would it be?

_____

_____

_____

_____

_____

_____

_____

_____

_____

_____

_____

_____

_____

_____

"I was quiet, but I was not blind."
- Jane Austen

Day 176: _____

If a psychic could tell you what will happen
in the future, what would you want to know?

_____

_____

_____

_____

_____

_____

_____

_____

_____

_____

_____

_____

_____

_____

"We need not be afraid of the future, for the future will be in our own hands."
- Thomas Dewey

Day 177: _____

What's one small thing you can do today
to protect the natural environment?

_____

_____

_____

_____

_____

_____

_____

_____

_____

_____

_____

_____

*"Treat the earth well; it was not given to you by
your parents, it was loaned to you by your children."*
- Native American proverb

Day 178: _____

Can you be counted on to do what
you say you'll do? Why or why not?

_____

_____

_____

_____

_____

_____

_____

_____

_____

_____

_____

_____

_____

_____

"Ability is important in our quest for success, but dependability is crucial."
- Zig Ziglar

Day 179: _____

What are some words you can use to describe
yourself? Were they all positive, negative or both?
Why did you chose these words?

_____

_____

_____

_____

_____

_____

_____

_____

_____

_____

_____

_____

"Be yourself, because an original is worth more than a copy."
- Unknown

Day 180: _____

What are some of the silliest things you've ever done?
Reflect upon the magic of spontaneity and laughter.

_____

_____

_____

_____

_____

_____

_____

_____

_____

_____

_____

_____

_____

_____

"There is nothing sillier than a silly laugh."
- Catullus

Day 181: _____

Spend an hour outside, whether its sitting on a
blanket on the grass or going for a walk, enjoy
the day if the weather permits. If not, save this
prompt for a sunny day and instead, write about
something that's been on your mind a lot lately.

_____

_____

_____

_____

_____

_____

_____

_____

_____

_____

_____

"All good things are wild and free."
- Henry David Thoreau

Day 182: _____

What's something you highly doubt about yourself? How can you overcome this doubt? What's a small step you can take in the next few days that will get you started?

_____

_____

_____

_____

_____

_____

_____

_____

_____

_____

_____

_____

"Doubt kills more dreams than failure ever will."
- Karim Seddiki

Day 183: _____

Start off the day with your favorite hot beverage.
Make a list of all the things you would like to
accomplish today. If these tasks are high priority,
make note of that. When you are finished, write about
how achieving these tasks made you feel. Are you
satisfied? If you didn't finish, how can you make time
for this task tomorrow? Was there something you
could have done differently?

_____

_____

_____

_____

_____

_____

_____

_____

_____

"The triumph of anything is a matter of organization."
- Kurt Vonnegut

Day 184: _____

If you have had "Ah Ha" moments, describe
your experience of a new realization of
yourself. If not, describe what things you wish
you understood more about yourself.

_____

_____

_____

_____

_____

_____

_____

_____

_____

_____

_____

"The unexamined life is not worth living."
- Socrates

Day 185: _____

How do you feel if you don't get something you have worked really hard for?

_____

_____

_____

_____

_____

_____

_____

_____

_____

_____

_____

_____

"Every problem has in it the seeds of its own solution.
If you don't have any problems, you don't get any seeds."
- Norman Vincent Peale

Day 186: _____

Challenge yourself and your friends today to be less wasteful and more conserving of resources like water, electricity, etc. See if you can run the water less while brushing your teeth, showering, cooking, etc. Make it a point to turn off 3 lights that aren't needed in your living/working space over the course of the day.

_____

_____

_____

_____

_____

_____

_____

_____

_____

_____

"The earth provides enough to satisfy every
man's needs, but not every man's greed."
- Gandhi

Day 187: _____

Take a 30 minute to an hour nap today. Write about how you feel after waking up. Do you nap often? Do you like taking naps? Can this be added into your routine? Why or why not?

_____

_____

_____

_____

_____

_____

_____

_____

_____

_____

_____

_____

"Learn from yesterday, live for today, look to tomorrow, rest this afternoon."
- Charles M. Schulz

Day 188: _____

How often do you step back and reflect upon the
way you are living and where you are headed?
What is one thing that is working well for you and
what's one thing that needs changing? Why?

_____

_____

_____

_____

_____

_____

_____

_____

_____

_____

"By three methods we may learn wisdom: First, by reflection,
which is noblest; Second, by imitation, which is easiest;
and third by experience, which is the bitterest."
- Confucius

Day 189: _____

If you could meet anyone in the world,
who would it be and why?

_____

_____

_____

_____

_____

_____

_____

_____

_____

_____

_____

_____

_____

_____

_____

"We meet the people we're supposed to when the time is just right."
- Alyson Noel

Day 190: _____

Do you get enough sleep at night? If not, what could you do to improve the quality and quantity of your sleep? If so, what do you do to relax?

_____

_____

_____

_____

_____

_____

_____

_____

_____

_____

_____

_____

_____

"Sleep is the golden chain that ties health and our bodies together."
- Thomas Dekker

Day 191: _____

What does your inner dialogue sound like?
Change your unwanted dialogue to a positive
dialogue and repeat it out loud 3 times today
to create new neural pathways.

_____

_____

_____

_____

_____

_____

_____

_____

_____

_____

_____

"Be the change you wish to see in the world."
- Mahatma Gandhi

Day 192: _____

How would you react if your friends honestly shared how they felt about you? How would you feel about sharing your honest feelings with your friends?

_____

_____

_____

_____

_____

_____

_____

_____

_____

_____

_____

_____

"Better a cruel truth than a comfortable delusion."
- Edward Abbey

Day 193: _____

How comfortable or uncomfortable are you
when you are completely alone? How can you
embrace being with yourself in a positive way?

_____

_____

_____

_____

_____

_____

_____

_____

_____

_____

_____

_____

"You cannot be lonely if you like the person you're alone with."
- Wayne Dyer

Day 194: _____

Which emotion do you experience the most?
What is this emotion telling you about yourself?

_____

_____

_____

_____

_____

_____

_____

_____

_____

_____

_____

_____

_____

"We either make ourselves happy or miserable.
The amount of work is the same."
- Carlos Castaneda

Day 195: _____

What was your biggest learning moment this week?

_____

_____

_____

_____

_____

_____

_____

_____

_____

_____

_____

_____

_____

_____

"There are no secrets to success. It is the result
of preparation, hard work, and learning from failure."
- Colin Powell

Day 196: _____

A mandala, like the one shown below, is often used to represent the universe. What contributions do you bring to the universe each day? How can small actions impact the world on a larger scale? Feel free to get in touch with your creative side, and decorate your 'universe'!

"He who lives in harmony with himself, lives in harmony with the universe."
- Marcus Aurelius

Day 197: _____

What ignites your spirit and excites you?

_____

_____

_____

_____

_____

_____

_____

_____

_____

_____

_____

_____

"Rest when you're weary. Refresh and renew yourself, your body, your mind, your spirit. Then get back to work."
- Ralph Marston

Day 198: _____

What are you passionate about? How often
do you express this passion and in what ways?

_____

_____

_____

_____

_____

_____

_____

_____

_____

_____

_____

_____

_____

"We are each gifted in a unique and important way. It is our
privilege and our adventure to discover our own special light."
- Mary Dunbar

Day 199: _____

Name 3 things that irritate you.
How can you cope when this feeling arises?

_____

_____

_____

_____

_____

_____

_____

_____

_____

_____

_____

_____

_____

"Just like children, emotions heal when they are heard and validated."
- Jill Bolte Taylor

Day 200: _____

Reflect again upon what it means to be the "best person you can be." How have you grown since you reflected upon this on Day 100 in your *Daily Brew Journal*?

_____

_____

_____

_____

_____

_____

_____

_____

_____

_____

_____

_____

"Be a first rate version of yourself, not a second rate version of someone else."
- Judy Garland

Day 201: _____

How would you describe your social life?
Are you satisfied with this aspect of your life?

_____

_____

_____

_____

_____

_____

_____

_____

_____

_____

_____

_____

*"A healthy social life is found only, when in the mirror
of each soul the whole community finds its reflection, and
when in the whole community the virtue of each one is living."*
- Rudolf Steiner

Day 202: _____

Look into your eyes in the mirror and tell yourself, "I love you _____(your name) and I accept you completely just the way you are." Repeat this exercise 3 times. Initially you may feel awkward… Do this to work toward feeling more comfortable loving yourself.

_____

_____

_____

_____

_____

_____

_____

_____

_____

_____

_____

"Love is the great miracle cure."
- Louise Hay

Day 203: _____

Do you have a healthy balance between alone
time and social life? Why or why not?

_____

_____

_____

_____

_____

_____

_____

_____

_____

_____

_____

_____

_____

_____

_____

"It is far better to be alone, than to be in bad company."
- George Washington

Day 204: _____

Instead of a 'to-do list,' try making a 'done list'
of everything you accomplished today.

_____

_____

_____

_____

_____

_____

_____

_____

_____

_____

_____

_____

_____

_____

"The best preparation for tomorrow is doing your best today."
- H. Jackson Brown Jr.

Day 205: _____

How can you improve your ability to really listen to someone with whom you regularly communicate?

_____

_____

_____

_____

_____

_____

_____

_____

_____

_____

_____

_____

_____

"The deepest feeling always shows itself in silence."
- Marianne Moore

Day 206: _____

Spend more time today with supportive
people and less time with unsupportive
people. Write about the awareness you've
gained in choosing people in your life.

_____

_____

_____

_____

_____

_____

_____

_____

_____

_____

_____

_____

"It's not just the tea... but where you are and with whom you enjoy it..."
- Robert Brink

Day 207: _____

What is your favorite physical aspect about yourself?
What about in others? Do you compare yourself to
others often? Do you think this is healthy?

_____

_____

_____

_____

_____

_____

_____

_____

_____

_____

_____

"If you don't love yourself, you'll always be
chasing after people who don't love you either."
- Mandy Hale

Day 208: _____

What are some of your triggers? How can knowing your own triggers help you in an uncomfortable situation? Observe your behavior today and notice a time you were triggered and write about how today's experience was different than the past.

_____

_____

_____

_____

_____

_____

_____

_____

_____

_____

_____

"We are not a victim of our emotions or thoughts. We can understand our triggers and use them as tools to help us respond more objectively."
- Elizabeth Thornton

Day 209: _____

Do you have any unmet needs? If so, what
are they and how can these needs be met?

_____

_____

_____

_____

_____

_____

_____

_____

_____

_____

_____

_____

_____

_____

_____

"Healing is not linear."
- Anonymous

Day 210: _____

Make a list of things you dislike about yourself,
followed by a list of what you like most about
yourself. How do these lists compare?

_____

_____

_____

_____

_____

_____

_____

_____

_____

_____

_____

_____

"To fall in love with yourself is the first key to happiness."
- Robert Morley

Day 211: _____

What's a relaxation technique that you have
heard about but never tried? Meditation?
Mindfulness? Prayer? Yoga? Deep Breathing?
Pick one, watch a short video online about it and
see if it could work for you. Write below what
you liked/disliked about the one you picked.

_____

_____

_____

_____

_____

_____

_____

_____

_____

" 'Thank You' is the best prayer that anyone can say. I say that one
a lot. Thank you expresses extreme gratitude, humility, understanding."
- Alice Walker

Day 212: _____

If you were given a large amount of money to spend, what would you spend it on and why?

_____

_____

_____

_____

_____

_____

_____

_____

_____

_____

_____

_____

"Work like you don't need the money. Love like you've
never been hurt. Dance like nobody's watching."
- Satchel Paige

Day 213: _____

In what ways do you show yourself love?

_____

_____

_____

_____

_____

_____

_____

_____

_____

_____

_____

_____

_____

_____

_____

_____

"We can climb mountains with self-love."
- Samira Wiley

Day 214: _____

Listen to your favorite music today. Why
is this your favorite? What comes to mind
when writing about what you hear?

_____

_____

_____

_____

_____

_____

_____

_____

_____

_____

_____

"Music expresses that which cannot be said
and on which it is impossible to be silent."
- Victor Hugo

Day 215: _____

What is something you did this year that
you'll remember for the rest of your life?

_____
_____
_____
_____
_____
_____
_____
_____
_____
_____
_____
_____
_____
_____

"Some memories are unforgettable, remaining ever vivid and heartwarming!"
- Joseph B. Wirthlin

Day 216: _____

Write about a stressful event coming up. What can you do to help cope with this stress? Is this a positive coping mechanism? If not, what can you do to cope with this future event in a positive manner?

_____

_____

_____

_____

_____

_____

_____

_____

_____

_____

_____

"It's not stress that kills us, it is our reaction to it."
- Hans Seyle

Day 217: _____

What is something you enjoy doing when you're bored? Is this the best use of your time? Since too much of a good thing can be a bad thing, should you consider cutting back on this activity?

_____

_____

_____

_____

_____

_____

_____

_____

_____

_____

_____

_____

"A cure for boredom is curiosity. There is no cure for curiosity."
- Dorothy Parker

Day 218: _____

How much time and energy do you
spend to favorably impress other
people? How healthy is this use of time?

_____

_____

_____

_____

_____

_____

_____

_____

_____

_____

_____

_____

"We have to wake up. We have to refuse to be a clone."
- Alice Walker

Day 219: _____

Refrain from checking your social media
accounts today. How does this make
you feel? Was this a hard or easy task?

_____

_____

_____

_____

_____

_____

_____

_____

_____

_____

_____

_____

"Going back to a simpler life is not a step backward."
- Yvon Chouinard

Day 220: _____

Write the story you tell yourself about a
disappointment or perceived failure in your life.
Revise this story you tell yourself into a positive story.

_____

_____

_____

_____

_____

_____

_____

_____

_____

_____

_____

_____

"I do not fix problems. I fix my thinking. Then problems fix themselves."
- Louise Hay

Day 221: _____

If you could live anywhere in the world, where would it be? Would you live with someone else?

_____

_____

_____

_____

_____

_____

_____

_____

_____

_____

_____

_____

_____

_____

_____

"Your sacred space is where you can find yourself over and over again."
- Joseph Campbell

Day 222: _____

Have you made promises to others lately that you haven't kept? Do your actions line up with your words? Why or why not? Why are these things important?

_____

_____

_____

_____

_____

_____

_____

_____

_____

_____

_____

"Reliability creates credibility."
- Gerald Brooks

Day 223: _____

Who do you celebrate your victories with? Are there others who should hear about your successes?

_____

_____

_____

_____

_____

_____

_____

_____

_____

_____

_____

_____

_____

"There are victories of the soul and spirit. Sometimes, even if you lose, you win."
- Elie Wiesel

Day 224: _____

If you were fearless what would your life look like?

_____

_____

_____

_____

_____

_____

_____

_____

_____

_____

_____

_____

_____

_____

"Believe you can and you're halfway there."
- Theodore Roosevelt

Day 225: _____

When was a time that you made a positive impact
on someone's life? How did you go about doing
this and how did you feel afterward?

_____

_____

_____

_____

_____

_____

_____

_____

_____

_____

_____

_____

"We rise by lifting others."
- Robert Ingersoll

Day 226: _____

Discuss your dream job and why it would
make you feel fulfilled. What other aspects of
your life make you feel this way?

_____

_____

_____

_____

_____

_____

_____

_____

_____

_____

_____

_____

_____

_____

"If you have a heartbeat, there's still time for your dreams."
- Sean Stephenson

Day 227:_____

How do you define "friendship"? How does a friend differ from an acquaintance? How many of each do you have in your life at present? Would you like these numbers to change? Why or why not?

_____

_____

_____

_____

_____

_____

_____

_____

_____

_____

_____

_____

"A friend is one that knows you as you are, understands where you have been, accepts what you have become, and gently still allows you to grow."
- William Shakespeare

Day 228: _____

Write about a personal achievement you
take pride in. What steps did you have
to take in order to accomplish this?

_____

_____

_____

_____

_____

_____

_____

_____

_____

_____

_____

*"Achievement seems to be connected with action.
Men and women keep moving. They make mistakes but they don't quit."
- Conrad Hilton*

Day 229: _____

What was something you cherished when you
were a child? Do you still have this? Discuss
why this holds importance for you.

_____

_____

_____

_____

_____

_____

_____

_____

_____

_____

_____

_____

"Cherish youth, but trust old age."
- Proverb

Day 230: _____

Are you connected to technology too often?
How can you find a healthier balance between
technology and real, human interaction?

_____

_____

_____

_____

_____

_____

_____

_____

_____

_____

_____

"Turn off your email; turn off your phone; disconnect from the Internet; figure
out a way to set limits so you can concentrate when you need to, and disengage
when you need to. Technology is a good servant but a bad master."
- Gretchen Rubin

Day 231: _____

Do you believe in second chances? Why or why not?
Could this be a dealbreaker for you in a relationship?

_____

_____

_____

_____

_____

_____

_____

_____

_____

_____

_____

_____

_____

_____

"Life is change. Growth is optional. Choose wisely."
- Karen Kaiser Clark

Day 232: _____

What would you like to see more of in your life?

_____

_____

_____

_____

_____

_____

_____

_____

_____

_____

_____

_____

_____

_____

"It is not in the pursuit of happiness that we
find fulfillment, it is in the happiness of pursuit."
- Denis Waitley

Day 233: _____

Say thank you to someone who did something
kind for you today. If you did something kind
for yourself or someone else, say thank you to
yourself. How does this feel?

_____

_____

_____

_____

_____

_____

_____

_____

_____

_____

_____

"No act of kindness, no matter how small is ever wasted."

- Aesop

Day 234: _____

What's something you learned recently about yourself
or others that will help you in the future?

_____

_____

_____

_____

_____

_____

_____

_____

_____

_____

_____

_____

_____

"That is what learning is. You suddenly understand
something you've understood all your life, but in a new way."
- Doris Lessing

$\mathcal{D}$ay 235: _____

What is something you know
that you would rather not know?

_____

_____

_____

_____

_____

_____

_____

_____

_____

_____

_____

_____

*"To know that we know what we know, and to know that we
do not know what we do not know, that is true knowledge."*
- Nicolaus Copernicus

Day 236: _____

What is a goal you have set for yourself
this year? Write 3 steps you can take
towards achieving this goal.

_____

_____

_____

_____

_____

_____

_____

_____

_____

_____

_____

"By recording your dreams and goals on paper, you set in motion the process of becoming the person you most want to be. Put your future in good hands - your own."- Mark Victor Hansen

Day 237: _____

Reconnect this week with someone you have
been meaning to reach out to for a long time.
What feelings would you like to express?
Write about your reconnection experience.

_____

_____

_____

_____

_____

_____

_____

_____

_____

_____

_____

"Beautiful memories are like old friends. They may not
always be on your mind, but they are forever in your heart."
- Susan Gale

Day 238: _____

What side of you do few people get to see? Should you keep things this way or work to change it?

_____

_____

_____

_____

_____

_____

_____

_____

_____

_____

_____

_____

_____

_____

"Never let the opinions of others become the measure of your self-worth."
- Anonymous

Day 239: _____

What's something you're angry about?
How can you start the process of letting this go?

_____

_____

_____

_____

_____

_____

_____

_____

_____

_____

_____

_____

_____

_____

"An eye for an eye only ends up making the whole world blind."
- Mahatma Gandhi

Day 240: _____

How important is adventure in your life?
What's the last adventure you participated in
and what does your next adventure entail? If
you don't have an adventure planned, should
you begin planning one? Why or why not?

_____

_____

_____

_____

_____

_____

_____

_____

_____

_____

_____

"We must go and see for ourselves."
- Jacques Cousteau

Day 241: _____

What is the top priority in your life right now?
Is there more than one? How do you balance
this with the other aspects of your life?

_____

_____

_____

_____

_____

_____

_____

_____

_____

_____

_____

_____

"Balance is not something you find, it's something you create."
- Jana Kingsford

Day 242: _____

If you could do anything in the world
without failing, what would you do?

_____

_____

_____

_____

_____

_____

_____

_____

_____

_____

_____

_____

_____

"Anyone who has never made a mistake has never tried anything new."
- Albert Einstein

Day 243: _____

Who is the most inspiring
person you've ever met and why?

_____

_____

_____

_____

_____

_____

_____

_____

_____

_____

_____

"...But a role model in the flesh provides more than inspiration; his or her very existence is confirmation of possibilities one may have every reason to doubt, saying, 'Yes, someone like me can do this.'"
- Sonia Sotomayor

Day 244: _____

What does "finding inner peace" mean? What does it or what would it look like and feel like for you?

_____

_____

_____

_____

_____

_____

_____

_____

_____

_____

_____

_____

_____

_____

"Silence isn't empty, it's full of answers."
- Unknown

Day 245: _____

In what ways have hard times and challenging situations made you a better person?

_____

_____

_____

_____

_____

_____

_____

_____

_____

_____

_____

_____

"The journey is never ending. There's always going to be growth, adversity, improvement."
- Antonio Brown

Day 246: _____

Think of a time when you wanted to be like someone else. Why did you want to be like this person? How does this compare to who you are today?

_____

_____

_____

_____

_____

_____

_____

_____

_____

_____

_____

"Don't compare yourself to others. There's no comparison
between the sun and the moon. They shine when it's their time."
- Akinleye Isaac

Day 247: _____

What parts of your personality are you
most proud of? In what ways do these
traits influence how others see you?

_____

_____

_____

_____

_____

_____

_____

_____

_____

_____

_____

"People often say this or that person has not yet found himself.
But the self is not something one finds, it is something one creates."
- Thomas Szasz

Day 248: _____

If you are in a bad mood, do you prefer to be left alone or have someone to cheer you up? Explain these feelings.

_____

_____

_____

_____

_____

_____

_____

_____

_____

_____

_____

_____

"When I wake up in a bad mood, I try not to stay in one.
Learn to make the best of what you have."
- Faith Hill

Day 249: _____

What changes would you like to see in
yourself within the next 3 to 4 weeks?
Is this a realistic goal?

_____

_____

_____

_____

_____

_____

_____

_____

_____

_____

_____

"Difficulty creates the opportunity for self-reflection and compassion."
- Suzan-Lori Parks

Day 250: _____

What are some things you wish you could have said yes to? How would this have changed your life now?

_____

_____

_____

_____

_____

_____

_____

_____

_____

_____

_____

_____

_____

_____

_____

"Creativity in life is about saying yes to new ideas."
- Nolan Bushnell

Day 251: _____

What is something you are grateful for this week?
Why?

_____

_____

_____

_____

_____

_____

_____

_____

_____

_____

_____

"A grateful heart is a beginning of greatness. It is an expression of humility.
It is a foundation for the development of such virtues as prayer, faith, courage,
contentment, happiness, love, and well-being."
- James E. Faust

Day 252: _____

Write for ten minutes, beginning with, "If ____ hadn't happened, I ____" Let whatever comes up, come up.

_____

_____

_____

_____

_____

_____

_____

_____

_____

_____

_____

_____

"Acceptance of what has happened is the first step
to overcoming the consequences of any misfortune."
- William James

Day 253: _____

Identify the qualities that make you lovable.

_____

_____

_____

_____

_____

_____

_____

_____

_____

_____

_____

_____

_____

*"By being yourself, you put something wonderful
in the world that was not there before."*
- Edwin Elliot

Day 254: _____

Recount some ways in which you have
helped others. Use this time to reflect on
how helping others affects your mood.

_____

_____

_____

_____

_____

_____

_____

_____

_____

_____

_____

_____

_____

"Look for a way to lift someone up. And if that's all you do, that is enough."
· Elizabeth Lesser

Day 255: _____

If you chose one thing that would never
change, what would it be and why?

_____

_____

_____

_____

_____

_____

_____

_____

_____

_____

_____

_____

_____

"Better to be the one who smiled than the one who didn't smile back."
- Marie Gayatri Stein

Day 256: _____

Identify when you will need to use
coping skills. Which techniques have
been the most helpful in the past?

_____

_____

_____

_____

_____

_____

_____

_____

_____

_____

_____

"We have two strategies for coping;
the way of avoidance or the way of attention."
- Marilyn Ferguson

Day 257: _____

What is something you are looking
forward to? How important is it to have
something to look forward to?

_____

_____

_____

_____

_____

_____

_____

_____

_____

_____

_____

_____

"What you seek is seeking you."
- Rumi

Day 258: _____

Write about an event that has changed you...
positive or negative.

_____

_____

_____

_____

_____

_____

_____

_____

_____

_____

_____

_____

_____

*"If you're going to ask yourself life-changing questions,
be sure to do something with the answers."*
- Bo Bennett

Day 259: _____

What is the most unique thing about you?
Do you like to hide it or let it show? Why?

_____

_____

_____

_____

_____

_____

_____

_____

_____

_____

_____

_____

_____

"You have to be odd to be number one."
- Dr. Seuss

Day 260: _____

What is the greatest accomplishment of your life so far? Is there anything you hope to do that is even better? What are a few first steps you could take to begin accomplishing this future goal?

_____

_____

_____

_____

_____

_____

_____

_____

_____

_____

_____

_____

"Discipline is the bridge between goals and accomplishment"
- Jim Rohn

Day 261: _____

Create your own prompt today while exploring your own creativity with this intricate image!

"Tomorrow is the most important thing in life. Comes into us at midnight very clean. It's perfect when it arrives and it puts itself in our hands. It hopes we've learned something from yesterday."
- John Wayne

Day 262: _____

What healthy habits would you like to cultivate? Set realistic goals for one or some of your healthy new habits goals. Choose one to begin today and make it happen.

_____

_____

_____

_____

_____

_____

_____

_____

_____

_____

_____

_____

"Our bodies are our gardens - our wills are our gardeners."
- William Shakespeare

Day 263: _____

Where do you most want to travel? Can you make this happen? If not, what's a place that is more realistic to visit? What do you hope or expect to gain from this experience?

_____

_____

_____

_____

_____

_____

_____

_____

_____

_____

_____

_____

"Once a year, go someplace you've never been."
- Dalai Lama XIV

Day 264: _____

What are some things you wish you could have said no to? How would this have changed your life now?

_____

_____

_____

_____

_____

_____

_____

_____

_____

_____

_____

_____

_____

_____

"Saying no can be the ultimate self-care."
- Claudia Black

Day 265: _____

Write and send an email, note or letter of
support to someone going through a hard time.

_____

_____

_____

_____

_____

_____

_____

_____

_____

_____

_____

_____

_____

"The best love is the kind that awakens the soul; that makes us reach for more,
that plants the fire in our hearts and brings peace to our minds."
- Nicholas Sparks

Day 266: _____

If you've suffered as a result of someone else's actions, write about the event from his or her perspective. What was his/her back story and what was going on in his/her life at the time? What does forgiving another person mean, and what would it take for you to forgive him or her?

_____

_____

_____

_____

_____

_____

_____

_____

_____

_____

"The wound is the place where the light enters you."
- Rumi

Day 267: _____

Whom do you admire the most?
How has this person inspired you?

_____

_____

_____

_____

_____

_____

_____

_____

_____

_____

_____

_____

_____

"Choose to focus your time, energy and conversation around people who inspire you, support you and help you to grow you into your happiest, strongest, wisest self."
- Karen Salmansohn

Day 268: _____

Describe a situation where everything
worked out for you. What role did you
play in creating this postive outcome?

_____

_____

_____

_____

_____

_____

_____

_____

_____

_____

_____

_____

_____

"Do not let the behavior of others destroy your inner peace."
- Dalai Lama XIV

Day 269: _____

Are you confrontational? Do you find this is a helpful tactic for you when conquering difficult situations? Why or why not?

_____

_____

_____

_____

_____

_____

_____

_____

_____

_____

_____

"In your life, you go through a difficult situation or a very good situation, and you have different moods, but you learn things from your experiences."
- Fernando Torres

278 ❦ THE DAILY BREW

Day 270: _____

Describe how you want your life
to look in 5, 10 and 15 years.

_____

_____

_____

_____

_____

_____

_____

_____

_____

_____

_____

_____

_____

"What's coming will come, and we'll meet it when it does."
- Hagrid

Day 271: _____

If you could change one thing that people
misunderstand about you, what would that be?
What positive change(s) would happen as a result?

_____

_____

_____

_____

_____

_____

_____

_____

_____

_____

_____

_____

"It is better to understand little than to misunderstand a lot."
- Anatole France

Day 272: _____

What activities bring out your inner child?
Do you engage in these often enough?

_____

_____

_____

_____

_____

_____

_____

_____

_____

_____

_____

_____

_____

_____

"Always be on the lookout for the presence of wonder."
- E. B. White

Day 273: _____

My 3 greatest qualities are...

_____

_____

_____

_____

_____

_____

_____

_____

_____

_____

_____

_____

_____

_____

_____

_____

*"Plant your own garden and decorate your own soul
instead of waiting for someone to bring you flowers."*
- Jorge Luis Borges

Day 274: _____

What are 3 things about your past
that you are most thankful for?

_____

_____

_____

_____

_____

_____

_____

_____

_____

_____

_____

_____

_____

_____

"In everything, give thanks."
- 1 Thessalonians 5:18

Day 275: _____

When you know you have a lot of things to do,
do you tend to tackle them immediately, or do
you prefer to procrastinate? Why?

_____

_____

_____

_____

_____

_____

_____

_____

_____

_____

_____

_____

_____

_____

"You don't have to see the whole staircase. Just take the first step."
- Martin Luther King Jr.

Day 276: _____

Proper hydration can help our mood, stamina, stress resistance and more. Do you drink enough water each day? If not, will you commit to increasing your daily intake of water? Should you carry a water bottle with you to make sure you drink enough water each day? What other reminders might work for you?

_____

_____

_____

_____

_____

_____

_____

_____

_____

_____

"Drinking water is essential to a healthy lifestyle."
- Stephen Curry

Day 277: _____

Is there anything you see in your personality that you don't understand? Write about this with an eye towards trying to explain where it comes from, even if it's only a theory or a guess.

_____

_____

_____

_____

_____

_____

_____

_____

_____

_____

_____

_____

"Knowing yourself is the beginning of all wisdom."
- Aristotle

Day 278: _____

What is the greatest responsibility you have?
How well are you doing balancing this
responsibility with other areas of your life?

_____

_____

_____

_____

_____

_____

_____

_____

_____

_____

_____

"We are made wise not by the recollection of our past,
but by the responsibility for our future."
- George Bernard Shaw

Day 279: _____

In what ways can you choose peace
over conflict in your relationships?

_____

_____

_____

_____

_____

_____

_____

_____

_____

_____

_____

_____

_____

"Blessed are the Peace-Makers for they shall be called the Children of God."-
Mathew 5:9

Day 280: _____

What would constitute a "perfect" day for you? Why?

_____

_____

_____

_____

_____

_____

_____

_____

_____

_____

_____

_____

_____

_____

"Where there is love there is life."
- Mahatma Gandhi

Day 281: _____

How would you describe yourself to a stranger?

_____

_____

_____

_____

_____

_____

_____

_____

_____

_____

_____

_____

_____

_____

"What you think, you become."
- Buddha

Day 282: _____

Describe the last time you handled something unexpected well. What coping skills did you use that you could use the next time the unexpected happens?

_____

_____

_____

_____

_____

_____

_____

_____

_____

_____

_____

_____

_____

_____

"Sometimes the most scenic roads in life are the detours you didn't mean to take."
- Angela N. Blount

Day 283: _____

In what ways have you possibly settled for less than your worth? Write about how you have changed regarding your self-worth.

_____

_____

_____

_____

_____

_____

_____

_____

_____

_____

_____

_____

_____

"You. Are. Enough."
- Unknown

Day 284: _____

What is your favorite hobby? Do you do it often
enough? If not, what can you do to change this?

_____

_____

_____

_____

_____

_____

_____

_____

_____

_____

_____

"Climb the mountain; not to plant your flag, but to embrace
the challenge, enjoy the air, and behold the view; climb it so
you can see the world, not so the world can see you."
- David McCullough Jr.

Day 285: _____

What limiting beliefs do you have that are
preventing you from achieving your goals?
Write down 3 limiting beliefs on a piece of paper
and discard this paper in a way you see fit while
saying good-bye forever to them. Write new
beliefs to replace the old beliefs and place them
somewhere where you will be reminded each
day of the new person you are becoming.

_____

_____

_____

_____

_____

_____

_____

_____

_____

_____

"Everything in your life is there as a vehicle for your transformation. Use it!"
- Ram Dass

Day 286: _____

What kinds of energy do you often
attract from others? Is this similar or
different from the energy you put forth?

_____

_____

_____

_____

_____

_____

_____

_____

_____

_____

_____

_____

"Slow down. Be intentional. Notice the energy
you are bringing into this space and moment."
- Brendan Burchard

Day 287: _____

Draw a picture or write about one of your favorite places. Why is this place special to you?

> "Broken crayons still color."
> - Anonymous

Day 288: _____

Is your personal confidence too dependent
on the opinion of others? Why or why not?

_____

_____

_____

_____

_____

_____

_____

_____

_____

_____

_____

_____

"Confidence is not: 'they will like me.'
Confidence is: 'I'll be fine if they don't'."
- Mandy Hale

Day 289: _____

Is there anyone you keep meaning to make plans with? Is there someone you haven't talked to in a while? Today, make it a point to reach out to one of these people.

_____

_____

_____

_____

_____

_____

_____

_____

_____

_____

_____

"If things start happening, don't worry, don't stew.
Just go right along, and you'll start happening too."
- Dr. Seuss

Day 290: _____

Think of a person who you find annoying. What traits do they possess that irritate you the most? Is there anything you can do to focus more on their positive attributes or to see them in a better light?

_____

_____

_____

_____

_____

_____

_____

_____

_____

_____

_____

"Everything that irritates us about others can lead us to an understanding of ourselves."
- Carl Jung

Day 291: _____

A positive affirmation is a short statement that can be
used for personal improvement. What is a positive
affirmation you can apply in your own life?

_____

_____

_____

_____

_____

_____

_____

_____

_____

_____

_____

_____

"We must concentrate not merely on the negative
expulsion of war but the positive affirmation of peace".
- Martin Luther King, Jr.

Day 292: _____

When do you feel most vulnerable? How can you feel more secure during these times?

_____

_____

_____

_____

_____

_____

_____

_____

_____

_____

_____

_____

_____

"Vulnerability sounds like truth and feels like courage.
Truth and courage aren't always comfortable, but they're never weakness."
- Brené Brown

Day 293: _____

What do you do for fun? How often do you
have fun? Make a plan today for fun times
in your life in the next week.

_____

_____

_____

_____

_____

_____

_____

_____

_____

_____

_____

_____

"If you obey all of the rules, you miss all of the fun."
- Katherine Hepburn

Day 294: _____

What parts of your life are you avoiding?
What is the underlying fear in you that keeps
you in the avoidance mode? What are steps
you can take to move through the fear?

_____

_____

_____

_____

_____

_____

_____

_____

_____

_____

_____

"*What you resist, persists.*"
- *Carl G. Jung*

Day 295: _____

What opportunities are you looking for?
How can you create these opportunities for yourself?

_____

_____

_____

_____

_____

_____

_____

_____

_____

_____

_____

_____

*"Opportunity is missed by most people because
it's dressed in overalls and looks like work."*
- Thomas Edison

Day 296: _____

Are you willing to let kindness from others into your heart? Why or why not?

_____

_____

_____

_____

_____

_____

_____

_____

_____

_____

_____

_____

_____

_____

"Kindness is a language which the deaf can hear and the blind can see."
- Mark Twain

Day 297: _____

What are you busy with today? Will this
matter 1 year from now? 3 years? 5 years?

_____

_____

_____

_____

_____

_____

_____

_____

_____

_____

_____

_____

_____

_____

_____

"Live as if you were to die tomorrow. Learn as if you were to live forever."
- Mahatma Gandhi

The Daily Do

Day 298: _____

Reflect upon a desire to make an important change in your life. How much effort will making this change take? Is it worth it? If yes, what's one small step you can take today to begin making this change?

_____
_____
_____
_____
_____
_____
_____
_____
_____
_____
_____
_____
_____

"When we are no longer able to change a situation,
we are challenged to change ourselves."
- Viktor Frankl

Day 299: _____

What do you believe you deserve?
Explain why you deserve this.

_____

_____

_____

_____

_____

_____

_____

_____

_____

_____

_____

*"Your value doesn't decrease based on
someone else's inability to see your worth."*
- Ted Rubin

Day 300: _____

Have you ever lost someone or something that meant a lot to you? How did you cope with the loss? Are you still grieving? How have you changed as a person as a result of this loss?

_____

_____

_____

_____

_____

_____

_____

_____

_____

_____

_____

_____

"Grief is in two parts. The first is loss. The second is the remaking of life."
- Anne Roiphe

Day 301: _____

For what in your life do you feel most grateful? Write
a letter of gratitude for all you are grateful for today.

_____

_____

_____

_____

_____

_____

_____

_____

_____

_____

_____

_____

_____

*"Every day, I like to wake up and remind
myself to be grateful of the simple things."*
- Miranda Kerr

Day 302: _____

What are your 3 best talents?

_____

_____

_____

_____

_____

_____

_____

_____

_____

_____

_____

_____

_____

"I think one of the keys to leadership is recognizing that everybody has gifts and talents. A good leader will learn how to harness those gifts toward the same goal."
- Ben Carson

Day 303: _____

In your ideal world, what would you like to see if you looked outside your window? Describe in detail.

_____

_____

_____

_____

_____

_____

_____

_____

_____

_____

_____

_____

"In an ideal world, I'd spend every weekend
at my home in Zermatt in Switzerland."
- Vanessa Mae

Day 304: _____

Have you ever wanted to do something good for the world but didn't know where to start? Is there a small thing you can do today to develop your idea?

_____

_____

_____

_____

_____

_____

_____

_____

_____

_____

_____

"Never doubt that a small group of thoughtful, committed, citizens can change the world. Indeed, it is the only thing that ever has."
- Margaret Mead

Day 305: _____

Are there any difficult decisions you are currently facing? How do you plan to make this decision? How have you made difficult choices in the past?

_____

_____

_____

_____

_____

_____

_____

_____

_____

_____

_____

_____

"You aren't what has happened to you, you are how you've overcome it."
- Beau Taplin

Day 306: _____

How do you deal with the uncertainty of life
and our inability to predict the future? Is your
style helping you or stressing you out more?

_____

_____

_____

_____

_____

_____

_____

_____

_____

_____

_____

"Embrace the uncertainty. Enjoy the beauty of becoming.
When nothing is certain, anything is possible."
- Mandy Hale

Day 307: _____

If I could meet anyone in the world
I would like to meet _____ because...

_____

_____

_____

_____

_____

_____

_____

_____

_____

_____

_____

_____

*"The meeting of two personalities is like the contact of two
chemical substances: if there is any reaction, both are transformed."*
- Carl Jung

Day 308: _____

During moments of stress or anxiety, what has been helpful for you in terms of coping with these emotions? Use the word search activity below to help brainstorm some healthy habits that you might find useful as coping techniques and methods of self-care.

```
D G U C T R S H O S E C V S D Q P I D R
Y R N N O S I H S H T E N L L N H U N A
E U I I U P S Y T O I H X E F V O P Z O
S A U V S G I J R W R T G E Y T T D N W
P X I M E W M N Z E W A K P K Z O I G X
N O I T A C A V G R S E W A R D G C K B
C O M M U N I T Y S E R V I C E R L W M
E J O U R N A L A H K B P M R O A Y I K
G T O I S J E M X T Z I O U S W P S R Y
P R A Y Q D W C N A M V L S Z A H C E C
N U R T D A N C E B I V W L F Z Y B Z T
P O R R I E X H A E X O W F S V L S W A
S J K M M D X T S N R N E D R A G E E L
P T R F E W E N Y D M O O J M T P W S K
M R R O E L G M S N K L M N F F U N F G
U L Y O X Q U O C F M U D G D W V W V M
A L Q U P H L O T K S G U X O L L A E Z
V V Y G P S O I O I M Y A P F L N L Z E
N F Q Q Z K O P C A I Z Z M E I E G A Y
W U U W V X T B B B A M L F E W G K R U
```

BATH
BREATHE
COMMUNITY
COPING SKILLS
CROSSWORDS
COOK
CRY
DANCE
DRAW
DRIVE
GARDEN
JOURNAL
MASSAGE
MEDITATE
MOVIES

MUSIC
PAINT
PHOTOGRAPHY
PRAY
PUZZLES
RUN
SERVICE
SHOWER
SING
SLEEP
SPORTS
TALK
VACATION
WALK
WRITE

Day 309: _____

Today, try consuming healthy snacks in between meals. Does your body feel more energized? How does snacking in between meals affect your mood? Is this something you will continue doing?

_____

_____

_____

_____

_____

_____

_____

_____

_____

_____

_____

"Eating good food is my favourite thing in the whole world. Nothing is more blissful."
- Justine Larbalestier

Day 310: _____

Do you act differently when you're around certain people? If so, why? Is this a positive or negative change? What does this tell you?

_____

_____

_____

_____

_____

_____

_____

_____

_____

_____

_____

"To be beautiful means to be yourself. You don't need to be accepted by others. You need to accept yourself."
- Thich Nhat Hahn

Day 311: _____

What has been stressful for you lately?
Was this within or outside of your control?

_____

_____

_____

_____

_____

_____

_____

_____

_____

_____

_____

_____

_____

_____

"Feelings are just visitors, let them come and go."
- Mooji

Day 312: _____

What is your usual way of handling stress? Is this a positive or negative way of coping? Is there anything about your approach to managing stress that needs to be changed? If not, do you give yourself enough credit for managing stress well?

_____

_____

_____

_____

_____

_____

_____

_____

_____

_____

"Resilience isn't a single skill. It's a variety of skills and coping mechanisms. To bounce back from bumps in the road as well as failures, you should focus on emphasizing the positive."
- Jean Chatzky

Day 313: _____

I am strong because…

"It is worth remembering that the time of greatest gain in terms of wisdom and inner strength is often that of greatest difficulty."
- Dalai Lama XIV

The Daily Do

Day 314: _____

When was the last time you allowed yourself
to enjoy a hot bath or shower? Make time to do
this today, while reflecting on your week and
any other thoughts that may be on your mind.
Towel off and write about any clarity you were
able to find during this time for yourself.

_____

_____

_____

_____

_____

_____

_____

_____

_____

_____

_____

"Noble deeds and hot baths are the best cure."
-Dodie Smith

Day 315: _____

Discuss positive and negative
interactions you've had in the past week.

_____

_____

_____

_____

_____

_____

_____

_____

_____

_____

_____

_____

_____

_____

_____

"Don't let the noise of others' opinions drown out your inner voice."
- Steve Jobs

Day 316: _____

What is the meaning of "trust" to you? Who do you trust and what qualities make them trustworthy?

_____

_____

_____

_____

_____

_____

_____

_____

_____

_____

_____

_____

_____

"A bird sitting on a tree is never afraid of the branch breaking, because her trust is not on the branch but on it's own wings. Always believe in yourself."
- Unknown

Day 317: _____

What should you do differently next year?

_____

_____

_____

_____

_____

_____

_____

_____

_____

_____

_____

_____

_____

_____

_____

"Only I can change my life. No one can do it for me."
- Carol Burnett

Day 318: _____

What 3 characteristics are you
looking for most in a partner?

_____

_____

_____

_____

_____

_____

_____

_____

_____

_____

_____

_____

_____

"Fill your paper with the breathings of your heart."
- William Wordsworth

Day 319: _____

In what ways might you be compromising
your own enjoyment of life?

_____

_____

_____

_____

_____

_____

_____

_____

_____

_____

_____

_____

_____

"Find a place inside where there's joy, and the joy will burn out the pain."
· Joseph Campbell

Day 320: _____

If money were no object, what would you rather be doing with your life? Is there anything you can realistically do to bring this to fruition? If not, what's a more realistic goal?

_____

_____

_____

_____

_____

_____

_____

_____

_____

_____

_____

_____

"Exploring the unknown requires tolerating uncertainty."
- Brian Greene

Day 321: _____

How do you deal with situations in which you don't get what you want or when you want it?

_____

_____

_____

_____

_____

_____

_____

_____

_____

_____

_____

_____

_____

"What you want and what you need aren't always the same. Be willing to delay short-term GRATIFICATION for long-term GREATNESS."
- Mandy Hale

Day 322: _____

Are you someone that conforms to everyone else's desire or do you stand your ground?

_____

_____

_____

_____

_____

_____

_____

_____

_____

_____

_____

_____

"Whether you think you can or think you can't, you are right."
- Henry Ford

Day 323: _____

If you have ever imagined yourself being famous describe what it looks like and why you are drawn to fame. If not, describe why you are not drawn to fame.

_____

_____

_____

_____

_____

_____

_____

_____

_____

_____

_____

_____

"Stay true in the dark and humble in the spotlight."
- Harold B. Lee

The Daily Do

Day 324: _____

Look at an old photograph.
What emotions do you feel about this memory?

_____

_____

_____

_____

_____

_____

_____

_____

_____

_____

_____

_____

_____

_____

"A photograph is the pause button of life."
- Ty Holland

Day 325: _____

What does "sense of purpose" mean to you?

_____

_____

_____

_____

_____

_____

_____

_____

_____

_____

_____

_____

_____

_____

_____

_____

"It's important to ask yourself, How am I useful to others? What do people want from me? That may very well reveal what you are here for."
- James Hillman

Day 326: _____

When was the last time you had to stick up for yourself? How did you go about doing this, and how did you feel afterwards?

_____

_____

_____

_____

_____

_____

_____

_____

_____

_____

_____

_____

"It takes a great deal of bravery to stand up to our enemies, but just as much to stand up to your friends."
- J. K. Rowling

Day 327: _____

What is something you have been trying to get rid of?
Write a goodbye letter to this person or thing that you
would like to release yourself from in the space below

_____

_____

_____

_____

_____

_____

_____

_____

_____

_____

_____

"Every day you must unlearn the ways that hold you back. You must rid yourself
of negativity, so you can learn to fly."
- Leon Brown

Day 328: _____

Have you ever experienced a break up? Ended
a difficult friendship? Are you satisfied with
the outcome? What did you learn about
yourself through this experience?

_____

_____

_____

_____

_____

_____

_____

_____

_____

_____

_____

"You can be a good person with a kind heart and still say no."
- Unknown

Day 329: _____

In what one-year period in your life do you feel you experienced the most personal growth. Why?

_____

_____

_____

_____

_____

_____

_____

_____

_____

_____

_____

_____

"I am learning every day to allow the space between where
I am and where I want to be, to inspire me and not terrify me."
- Tracee Ellis Ross

Day 330: _____

What are your goals? Long term? Short term?
Are these realistic and achievable?

_____

_____

_____

_____

_____

_____

_____

_____

_____

_____

_____

_____

_____

"Strive for progress, not perfection."
- Unknown

Day 331: _____

Do you think people misunderstand you?
Why and how?

_____

_____

_____

_____

_____

_____

_____

_____

_____

_____

_____

_____

_____

"Five minutes of communication can save
a year's worth of turmoil and misunderstanding."
- Joyce Meyer

Day 332: _____

If you had to pick one day to relive over and over for the rest of your life what would it be and why?

_____

_____

_____

_____

_____

_____

_____

_____

_____

_____

_____

"One of the best ways to make yourself happy in the present is to recall happy times from the past. Photos are a great memory-prompt, and because we tend to take photos of happy occasions, they weight our memories to the good." - Gretchen Rubin

Day 333: _____

Reflect upon a dream you've imagined for a
long time or a dream you are now imagining.
Describe the dream and how you envision you
will realize the dream or not? Why or why not?

_____

_____

_____

_____

_____

_____

_____

_____

_____

_____

*"Follow your bliss and the universe will open
doors for you where there were only walls."*
- Joseph Campbell

Day 334: _____

Take a few minutes and look up meditation videos.
Meditate for a couple of minutes. How did this make
you feel? Is it something you would do again?

_____

_____

_____

_____

_____

_____

_____

_____

_____

_____

_____

"Meditation can help us embrace our worries, our fear, our anger, and that is
very healing. We let our own natural capacity of healing do the work."
- Thich Nhat Hanh

Day 335: _____

What are some changes you've made within
the past 6 months? What changes would you
like to make within the next 6 months?.

_____

_____

_____

_____

_____

_____

_____

_____

_____

_____

_____

"The secret of change is to focus all your
energy not on fighting the old, but building the new."
- Socrates

Day 336: _____

Are you emotionally dependent on someone?
If so, who and why?

_____

_____

_____

_____

_____

_____

_____

_____

_____

_____

_____

_____

"I am no bird; and no net ensnares me;
I am a free human being with an independent will."
- Charlotte Bronte

Day 337: _____

Write about a life changing experience that you have had. What have you learned from this experience?

_____

_____

_____

_____

_____

_____

_____

_____

_____

_____

_____

_____

_____

_____

"Have more than you show, speak less than you know."
- William Shakespeare

Day 338: _____

Take a few minutes and watch a video or two
of animals in the wild. Now, look up photos of
wild animals in their natural habitat.
Write briefly about how these make you feel.

_____

_____

_____

_____

_____

_____

_____

_____

_____

_____

_____

_____

"People are not going to care about animal conservation and the protection of
habitat unless they think animals are worthwhile and necessary to our survival."
· Anonymous

Day 339: _____

What would your ideal transformation look like? Is this realistic? If not, what can you do to make your goal more realistic? If so, what steps can you take to get to where you want to be?

_____

_____

_____

_____

_____

_____

_____

_____

_____

_____

_____

"Transformation literally means going beyond your form."
- Wayne Dyer

Day 340: _____

What things that you once thought would bring you happiness but didn't are you willing to let go of?

_____

_____

_____

_____

_____

_____

_____

_____

_____

_____

_____

_____

"We must let go of the life we have planned,
so as to accept the one that is waiting for us."
- Joseph Campbell

Day 341: _____

If you could achieve anything what would it be? Describe the feelings associated with this accomplishment.

_____

_____

_____

_____

_____

_____

_____

_____

_____

_____

_____

_____

_____

"The only person you are destined to become is the person you decide to be."
- Ralph Waldo Emerson

Day 342: _____

What are your most destructive habits? What are a few ways you could work on breaking these habits?

_____

_____

_____

_____

_____

_____

_____

_____

_____

_____

_____

_____

_____

_____

"Bad habits are easier to abandon today than tomorrow."
- Proverb

Day 343: _____

Write about an opportunity you let pass you by and why. Are there opportunities on the horizon you should be investigating?

_____

_____

_____

_____

_____

_____

_____

_____

_____

_____

_____

"Opportunities are usually disguised as hard work,
so most people don't recognize them."
- Ann Landers

Day 344: _____

What was your high and low today?

_____

_____

_____

_____

_____

_____

_____

_____

_____

_____

_____

_____

_____

_____

"You can't let the highs get too high and you can't let the lows get too low."
- Heather O'Reilly

Day 345: _____

What is something you wish
you could admit to yourself?

_____

_____

_____

_____

_____

_____

_____

_____

_____

_____

_____

_____

*"You've been criticizing yourself for years, and it hasn't worked. Try approving
of yourself and see what happens."*
- Louise Hay

Day 346: _____

Even brief road trips can satisfy our desire for new places and new experiences. What are you doing to plan your next adventure?

_____

_____

_____

_____

_____

_____

_____

_____

_____

_____

_____

_____

"Work, Travel, Save, Repeat."

- Anonymous

Day 347: _____

What is your biggest worry?

_____

_____

_____

_____

_____

_____

_____

_____

_____

_____

_____

_____

_____

_____

"If something is wrong, fix it if you can. But train yourself not to worry.
Worry never fixes anything."
- Mary Hemingway

Day 348: _____

Clean out your room and donate, recycle and throw out everything you don't need. How does it feel to get rid of these things?

_____

_____

_____

_____

_____

_____

_____

_____

_____

_____

_____

_____

"Clear your mind of clutter, congestion and conflict. Free your mind of unproductive, nonessential thoughts about yourself and your life."
- Anonymous

Day 349: _____

Describe your current living situation.
What would you change about this set up?

_____

_____

_____

_____

_____

_____

_____

_____

_____

_____

_____

_____

_____

"Happiness cannot be traveled to, owned, earned, worn or consumed. Happiness is the spiritual experience of living every minute with love, grace, and gratitude."
- Denis Waitley

Day 350: _____

Think of a person you have hurt and think of
a way you would like to ask for forgiveness.
Set an intention to make it happen and write
about what came up for you.

_____

_____

_____

_____

_____

_____

_____

_____

_____

_____

_____

"Where there is discord, may we bring harmony. Where there is error,
may we bring truth. Where there is doubt, may we bring faith.
And where there is despair, may we bring hope."
- St. Francis of Assisi

Day 351: _____

Today my victories were:

_____

_____

_____

_____

_____

_____

_____

_____

_____

_____

_____

_____

"If you take no risks, you will suffer no defeats.
But if you take no risks, you win no victories."
- Richard M. Nixon

Day 352: _____

Go to sleep early tonight. Write about how
you think you will feel in the morning.
Once you wake up, finish writing a journal
entry about how you actually felt.

_____

_____

_____

_____

_____

_____

_____

_____

_____

_____

_____

"Sleep is the best meditation."
- Dalai Lama XIV

Day 353: _____

What is something that drives you? Why?

_____

_____

_____

_____

_____

_____

_____

_____

_____

_____

_____

_____

_____

_____

_____

_____

"The truest drive comes from doing what you love."
- Peter Diamandis

The Daily Do

Day 354: _____

Spend 30 minutes outside today in the quietest, most natural place you can find. Breathe in and out deeply and be refreshed by the sights and sounds you take in. Write about this time.

_____

_____

_____

_____

_____

_____

_____

_____

_____

_____

"The Great Spirit is in all things: he is in the air we breathe.
The Great Spirit is our Father, but the Earth is our Mother.
She nourishes us; that which we put into the ground she returns to us."
- Big Thunder (Bedagi) Wabanaki, Algonquin.

Day 355: _____

Below, list the most important people in your life right now. Write about the reasons they are so important to you. Have you shared these reasons with them?

_____

_____

_____

_____

_____

_____

_____

_____

_____

_____

_____

"There's only one thing more precious than our time, and that's who we spend it with."
- Leo Christopher

Day 356: _____

When was the last time you cried? Why? Was this a good cry? Or bad? How did you feel after crying?

_____

_____

_____

_____

_____

_____

_____

_____

_____

_____

_____

_____

_____

_____

"Crying is cleansing. There's a reason for tears, happiness or sadness."
- Dionne Warwick

Day 357: _____

If I didn't _____, I would have
never learned _____.

_____

_____

_____

_____

_____

_____

_____

_____

_____

_____

_____

_____

_____

"Everyone and everything shows up in our life as a reflection of something that is happening inside us."
- Alan Cohen

Day 358: _____

Write a thank you letter to your biggest
supporter and send it to this person.
Write about your feelings during this process.

_____

_____

_____

_____

_____

_____

_____

_____

_____

_____

_____

_____

_____

"Surround yourself with people who are going to motivate and inspire you."
- Charles M. Marcus

Day 359: _____

Color in the mandala using your favorite colors. Reflect on your favorite activities and why they're meaningful to you.

"Tears of joy are like the summer rain drops pierced by sunbeams."
- Hosea Ballou

Day 360: _____

What does your ideal day look
like, from morning to night?

_____

_____

_____

_____

_____

_____

_____

_____

_____

_____

_____

_____

"You don't always need a plan. Sometimes you
just need to breathe, trust, let go, and see what happens."
- Mandy Hale

Day 361: _____

Clean up some clutter around your house.
How do you feel after cleaning?
Can cleaning become a form of stress relief?

_____

_____

_____

_____

_____

_____

_____

_____

_____

_____

_____

"The objective of cleaning is not just to clean,
but to feel happiness living within that environment."
- Marie Kondo

Day 362: _____

What fictional character do you believe you are most
like? In what ways do you share similar strengths?
Find an image of this character and print it out.
Put it somewhere you'll see it each day.

_____

_____

_____

_____

_____

_____

_____

_____

_____

_____

_____

*"If you will practice being fictional for a while, you will understand that fictional
characters are sometimes more real than people with bodies and heartbeats."*
- Richard Bach

Day 363: _____

How has fear of the unknown stopped you from making an important decision in your life? Are there ways that you can become more comfortable with taking reasonable risks?

_____

_____

_____

_____

_____

_____

_____

_____

_____

"I truly believe that everything that we do and everyone we meet is put in our path for a purpose. There are no accidents; if we're willing to pay attention to the lessons we learn, trust our positive instincts and not be afraid to take risks or wait for some miracle to come knocking at our door."
- Marla Gibbs

Day 364: _____

How has journaling helped you? Is this something you would continue doing? Would you recommend journaling to other people?

_____

_____

_____

_____

_____

_____

_____

_____

_____

_____

_____

"The starting point of discovering who you are, your gifts, your talents, your dreams, is being comfortable with yourself. Spend time alone. Write in a journal. Take long walks in the woods."
- Robin S. Sharma

Day 365: _____

Congratulations! You finished *The Daily Brew Journal!* Is there anything else you feel the need to say? Write about it.

_____

_____

_____

_____

_____

_____

_____

_____

_____

_____

_____

"You can't go back and change the beginning,
but you can start where you are and change the ending."
- C.S. Lewis

Notes

_____

_____

_____

_____

_____

_____

_____

_____

_____

_____

_____

_____

_____

_____

_____

_____

_____

Notes

_____

_____

_____

_____

_____

_____

_____

_____

_____

_____

_____

_____

_____

_____

_____

_____

Notes

_____

_____

_____

_____

_____

_____

_____

_____

_____

_____

_____

_____

_____

_____

_____

_____

_____

Notes

Notes

_____

_____

_____

_____

_____

_____

_____

_____

_____

_____

_____

_____

_____

_____

_____

_____

_____

Notes

Notes

Notes

Notes

_____

_____

_____

_____

_____

_____

_____

_____

_____

_____

_____

_____

_____

_____

_____

_____

Notes

_____

_____

_____

_____

_____

_____

_____

_____

_____

_____

_____

_____

_____

_____

_____

_____

CPSIA information can be obtained
at www.ICGtesting.com
Printed in the USA
FFHW020338291118
49695280-54084FF